GW00493644

## the Best of Age Grade Coaching excellence

## AN ESSENTIAL GUIDE FOR COACHES, PARENTS AND PLAYERS

PUBLISHED BY PassporttoSport.com

# TABLE OF CONTENTS

| | | | |
|---|---|---|---|
| Table of Contents | 2 | The Warm-Up | 68-71 |
| Introduction | 3 | Cooling Down | 72-73 |
| Positions | 4-7 | Upper Body Stretches | 74 |
| Gear | 8-9 | Lower Body Stretches | 75 |
| Rugby Terminology | 10-11 | Strength and Conditioning | 76-77 |
| Referees Hand Signals | 12-13 | Speed and Agility | 78-79 |
| Rules by Age Group | 14 | Core Conditioning | 80-83 |
| Regulations of Mini Rugby | 15-19 | Safety and Equipment | 84-85 |
| Rugby Ethos | 20-21 | Staging a Match | 86 |
| Nutrition | 22-25 | Medical Supplies | 87-88 |
| Supplements and Rugby | 26-27 | Sports Injuries | 89-91 |
| Sports Psychology | 28-30 | Concussion | 92-94 |
| Coaching Children with Special Needs | 31-33 | Coaches Essential Equipment | 95 |
| Principles First - Ethical Coaching | 34-35 | Players Attendance Sheet | 96 |
| Coaching Children's Rugby | 36 | Players Contact Details | 97 |
| Training through Games | 37 | Sample Training Planner | 98 |
| Playing the Game | 38 | Match Day Planner | 99 |
| Managing the Games | 39 | Match Day Report Sheet | 100 |
| Measuring Success | 40-41 | Match Observation Sheet | 101 |
| Child Welfare | 42 | Self-Evaluation Form | 102 |
| Bullying | 43 | Rugby Games for Age 5-9 | 103 |
| Rest and Recovery | 44 | Rugby Games for Age 10-13 | 117 |
| Rate of Exertion | 45 | Rugby Games for Age 14-16 | 127 |
| Animal Walks | 46-47 | Notes | 134 |
| The Coaching Ladder | 48-49 | | |
| Age 6-8 | 50-51 | | |
| Age 9-10 | 52-53 | | |
| Age 11-12 | 54-55 | | |
| Age 13-14 | 58-61 | | |
| Age 15-16 | 64-67 | | |

## WELCOME...

Welcome to **PASSPORT TO RUGBY**, an essential guide for everyone involved in age grade rugby, in particular coaches or potential coaches, players and parents.

We have distilled almost 25 years of experience at this level into a simple, easy-to-follow guide into every aspect of the game. This handy reference will help coaches, players and parents, whether at home or at pitch-side, to get the most out of their training, playing and development.

The guide combines decades of experience at mini and youth level with the most up-to-date thinking on issues such as training methods and professional nutrition practices.

It will give coaches the information they need to run a modern training session and design appropriate goals for their age groups from season to season. And it will help the players and their parents to understand the thinking behind certain training drills or strategies for improvement.

Most importantly, the focus is on the young players; our goal is to ensure they enjoy being part of the rugby community, that they have fun, and that they will come back again and again anxious to be the best they can be.

And for the parents, this guide can help to ensure your children learn to play the game in a safe and enjoyable environment.

We are certain this guide offers something to everyone involved in age grade rugby.

## ABOUT THE AUTHOR...

Aidan O'Reilly is certified by the Irish Rugby Football Union (IRFU) as a Conditioning Coach. He has worked with the Irish Women's Senior Rugby squad and as a Strength Coach with the Dublin Senior Hurling squad. He has a diploma in Physical Fitness Conditioning from Setanta College, is certified as a Level One Weight-lifting Coach, and is a member of the National Strength and Conditioning Association (NSCA).

## CREDITS...

Joe Culley for his work on editing and proof-reading. Gillian Reddy and her team at Pen House for the design and Derry Dillon for the excellent illustrations.

# POSITIONS

There are 15 positions in a full rugby team (see illustration page 6), eight Forwards in the pack, and seven Backs.

The eight forwards are broken into three rows.

The **Front Row** includes the Loosehead Prop (1), the Hooker (2), and the Tighthead Prop (3).
The **Second Row** consists of the two Locks (or Second Rows, 4 and 5).
The **Back Row** (or Loose Forwards) includes the Blindside Flanker (6), the No. 8, and the Openside Flanker (7).

The seven Backs can also be broken into groups.

**Half-backs:** these are the Scrum-half (9) and Outhalf (or Flyhalf, 10).
**Centres:** Inside Centre (12) and Outside Centre (13).
**Back Three:** the Left Wing (11) the Right Wing (14), and the Fullback (15).

When the opposing packs engage for a scrum, they align slightly to the left so that the Prop wearing No. 3 puts his head between those of the opposition's Nos. 1 and 2. Thus he is the 'tighthead', as he cannot move his head. The No. 1 is the 'loosehead' as he is still relatively free to manoeuvre.

The Flankers, the Nos. 6 and 7, are "blindside" and "openside". As the illustration shows how the Backs are aligned, the No. 6 is 'blind' in that they cannot see or immediately follow the likely line of play. The No. 7 is "open" because they can see everything unfold and immediately join in the action, whether attack or defence.

1: **LOOSEHEAD:** big and powerful, the primary role is to support the Hooker so that they can get a clean 'strike' on the ball when it is put into the scrum. The ball is always put in from this side, under their noses. They also lift the taller Locks in a lineout.

2: **HOOKER:** main duties are to win the ball when it is put into the scrum, and – generally – throw in to the lineout. They are often, in effect, standing on one leg, the left, in the scrum as they wait for the ball, which is why they are 'propped' up on each side.

The HOOKER –
normally throws into the Lineout

3: **TIGHTHEAD:** often the most powerful player on a team, and the anchor of the scrum. They are the fulcrum, and put pressure on the opposition Loosehead. The right side of the body does much of the work. Also lifts in the lineout.

4 and 5: **LOCKS:** tall and strong, main duties are to 'lock', or steady, the scrum and push forward, and to win the ball in the lineout or on a kick-off. The No. 4 is often the (relatively) shorter and bulkier of the pair, often packs down behind the tighthead, where most of the pressure comes through a scrum.

6: **BLINDSIDE:** like all the backrow players, needs to be both strong and quick and relish contact. The No. 6 is often the first line of defence when the opposition begins an attacking move. A fierce tackler, the player hits the rucks and mauls hard. Often a third jumper in a lineout.

7: **OPENSIDE:** in contrast to the Blindside, the No. 7 is often in the first wave of attack, supporting a break from the No. 8 or on the shoulder of the Inside Centre. Again, strong in the tackle, rucks and mauls, trying to win the ball on the ground.

8: **NO.8:** (no other title has evolved): like the Flankers, duties include steadying the scrum, tackling and supporting the Backs in attack. But the No. 8 has the added responsibility of securing possession at the base of the scrum and giving the Half-backs time and space to initiate an attack. Must have a good sense of where their team-mates are.

The LOCKS –
are usually Lineout jumpers

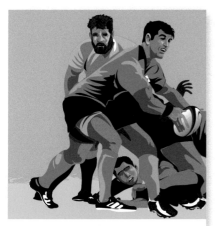

The SCRUMHALF –
Puts the Ball into the Scrum

9: **SCRUMHALF:** the link between the Forwards and the Backs. Put simply, the main role is to deliver the ball from the base of the scrum, ruck or maul to spark the backline. But the Scrumhalf is one of the prime decision-makers on the team, dictating pace of play, positioning and tactics. Needs excellent ball-handling and kicking skills. Also needs to be among the fittest and quickest in the team, as they must cover a huge amount of territory moving from scrum to ruck, breakdown to breakdown.

10: **OUTHALF:** the on field commander-in-chief, the prime decision-maker in the team, bossing both Forwards and Backs. They control the tempo of the game, alternating the method of attack, whether by running with the ball, moving it out along the backline or kicking ahead to turn the opposition. Aside from great skills, needs an almost instinctive ability to 'read' what's going on in the game. Generally the place-kicker. In the modern game, they must also be good tacklers.

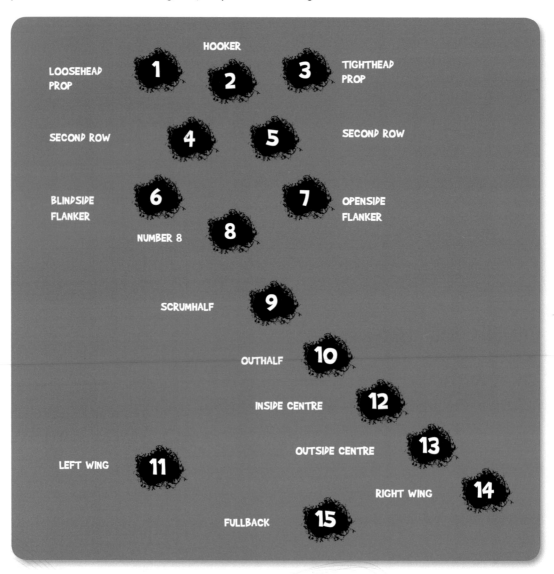

HOOKER

LOOSEHEAD PROP — 1

2

3 — TIGHTHEAD PROP

SECOND ROW — 4

5 — SECOND ROW

BLINDSIDE FLANKER — 6

7 — OPENSIDE FLANKER

NUMBER 8 — 8

SCRUMHALF — 9

OUTHALF — 10

INSIDE CENTRE — 12

OUTSIDE CENTRE — 13

LEFT WING — 11

RIGHT WING — 14

FULLBACK — 15

**The OUTHALF –
usually tasked with kicking duties**

**11 & 14: THE WINGERS:** traditionally – and still true – usually the quickest players in the team, but now no longer always the lightest. They are often at the end of an attacking move, but also often the last line of defence. In the modern game they are expected to be much more physical, hitting rucks and making numerous tackles. Good at catching a high kick.

**12: INSIDE CENTRE:** traditionally slightly stronger and quicker than the Outhalf, and often used to take the ball into first contact. Like the Outhalf, needs to know when to run and when to pass. Important defensive role in the middle of the field.

**13: OUTSIDE CENTRE:** traditionally was perhaps a bit quicker than the No.12, but plays essentially the same role.

**15: FULLBACK:** traditionally the last line of defence, the role has evolved into a greater attacking force. Good tacklers. Good at catching a high kick, and punting the ball a long way. Key skill is to anticipate the opposition's play. Now also needs the speed and skill to join in backline attacks.

**The FULLBACK –
must be good catching a high kick**

**The WINGERS –
traditionally the quickest players**

In the modern game many of the traditional roles of players have broken down. Now, Forwards are expected to handle the ball as well as Backs, while Backs are expected to be as physical and hard-tackling as Forwards. Everyone can do everything.

## RUGBY UNION EQUIPMENT GUIDE

As with any sport, rugby union requires a few pieces of specialist equipment. It is a physical, full-contact sport - so expect a few knocks while playing.

> " **But with the proper equipment, you can reduce the chances of injuries, as well as enjoy playing the game more** "

### GUM SHIELD

The gum shield is the most important piece of equipment a rugby player should own. It not only protects your teeth and gums, it can reduce damage around the jaw and the chances of getting concussed.

As every mouth is different, so every gum shield should be moulded to fit perfectly around the top half of the mouth. The best way to do this is to visit your dentist, who will make sure the shield is right for your mouth. The other type of gum shield is the popular "boil in the bag", which is moulded using hot water, and is available from most sports shops.

### HEAD PROTECTION

The most important thing to remember if you want to wear head protection is to make sure it is comfortable, otherwise it will only cause pain and injury. If you are a forward, make sure the cap does not cause problems in the scrum. If you can, scrum down with a friend when you are trying on different models, to make sure it fits properly.

### UPPER BODY PROTECTION

Upper body protection has been a feature of the sport for the past 20 years. The shoulders and the chest take much of the impact in tackles, so it's important these are well protected. Modern upper body protection is made from strong and lightweight material.

Again, comfort is the most important factor when considering chest protection. Make sure it fits you well, otherwise it will be not only uncomfortable on the field but will also increase your chance of picking up an injury. But remember, wearing body protection doesn't mean you are invincible and can do things others players can't – you'll do yourself more damage if you think like that.

## RUGBY SHIRTS

Rugby shirts need to be able to take plenty of tugging and pulling, while at the same time be lightweight, comfortable and strong.

Traditionally, jerseys were made from cotton, which would often get very heavy in the rain. But modern jerseys are made from lightweight, water-resistant synthetic fibres. Although your club/school will provide jerseys for matches, it is worth buying one for training.  Make sure it fits properly: too small and it will rip, too big and your opponents will be able to tackle you more easily. Some shirts at the top level are designed to be figure-hugging. They are lighter and designed to snap back when someone tries to grab them.

## RUGBY BOOTS

Rugby boots are similar to football boots, but have a higher cut designed to give extra support to the ankle.  However, more and more players – especially backs - prefer to use football-style boots, as the low cut allows for extra mobility. So it is important to understand what position you are playing before choosing which kind of boot you want.

Understand the shape of your feet and your running style. Find out whether you may be flat-footed or have a high arch.  Ideally, rugby boots will fit snugly, although if your feet are still growing then allow a little bit of room.

Also, different players prefer different fits. As forwards rely on lower-body strength for power in scrums, they need extra support around the ankle to help prevent foot injuries. Kickers prefer a tight-fitting boot because it gives them a better feel for the ball, while props like a high ankle cut for extra support in scrums. Wear the same type of socks you would wear on the pitch when you try on a boot for size.

Boots with screw-in studs are popular because players can adjust them depending on the conditions.  If the pitch is muddy, use a longer set of studs. When changing or tightening studs, put a bit of grease on the thread to prevent them from rusting.  Wearing the wrong kind of studs can do you - or a member of the opposition - a lot of harm. Referees will check whether your boots have any sharp edges or ridges, but it is also your duty to make sure your boots and studs are in good order.

## RUGBY BALL

A good quality ball will help you improve your handling and kicking skills on and off the field. In the old days, rugby balls were made of hand-stitched leather, which would get very heavy in the rain and were difficult to handle in slippery conditions.  The new waterproof materials make the ball much easier to handle in wet and muddy conditions.  Make sure your ball is properly pumped full of air before you start practising your passing, catching and kicking on your own or with a team-mate.

## KNOCK-ON

A knock-on occurs when a player loses possession of the ball and it goes forward, or when a player hits the ball forward with the hand or arm and the ball touches the ground, or another player, before the original player can catch it. If the ball goes forward off the leg or foot it is not a knock-on.

## RUCK

A ruck forms when one or more players from each team, who are on their feet and in physical contact, close around the ball on the ground. Players are rucking when they are using their feet – cleanly - to try to win or keep possession of the ball.

## MAUL

A maul begins when a player carrying the ball is held by one or more opponents, and one or more of the ball-carrier's team-mates bind on the ball-carrier. So, when it begins, a maul must have at least three players, all on their feet. All the players must be caught in or bound to the maul, and must be on their feet and still moving towards a goal line.

**" 5 points is awarded for a Try ... 2 points for a Conversion "**

## TACKLE

A tackle occurs when the ball-carrier is held by one or more opponents and is brought to ground. It is illegal to tackle an opponent above the shoulders, to tackle a player without the ball or to tackle a player who is in the air. These are considered dangerous and will be penalised.

An opposition player may not prevent the tackled player from passing the ball, or from releasing the ball and getting up or moving away from it. That's called 'killing the ball'. Also, no player may fall on or over the players lying on the ground after a tackle. Again, killing the ball.

## OFFSIDE

On the most fundamental level, the offside line in rugby is wherever the ball is. If your team is in possession, no player can be ahead of the teammate with the ball. However, offside can then get a bit complicated, as there are more specific rules relating to the scrum, lineout, ruck or maul.

When the ball is in a ruck, maul or scrum, any player who is in front of the hindmost foot of the hindmost player of the same side in the ruck/maul/scrum is offside.

When the ball is in a scrum, the opposing scrumhalf must stay behind the ball, and all the players **not** in the scrum must remain five metres behind the hindmost foot. In a lineout, players not forming part of the lineout, or acting as receiver, must stay at least 10 metres from the imaginary line on which the ball is thrown in.

A player who is offside may not interfere with play.

In particular, a player offside:
1. may not enter a ruck, maul or scrum
2. may not play the ball
3. may not move towards the ball
4. may not receive a pass (forward passes are illegal in any event)
5. may not move towards, tackle or obstruct a player of the opposing team who has the ball, or must move at least 10 metres away from any opponent who is waiting to receive the ball (for instance, waiting to catch a kick ahead)

Break any of these rules and a penalty will be awarded to the opposing team.

## "And 3 points is awarded for a Penalty"

### FOUL PLAY

Foul play is anything a player does that is against the letter and spirit of the Laws. It includes obstruction, unfair play, repeated infringements, dangerous play and misconduct.

Obstruction can include: charging or pushing, running in front of the ball-carrier, or blocking the tackler or the ball.

Unfair play includes: intentionally offending, time-wasting, or deliberately throwing the ball into touch.

Dangerous play includes: punching or striking, stamping, tripping, or dangerous tackling.

### KICK-OFF AND RESTARTS

These are taken from the halfway line. The player taking the kick (usually the number 10) must use a drop kick, and it must travel at least 10 metres.

For a comprehensive look at the Laws of the game, see the International Rugby Board website: www.irblaws.com

Throw forward/
forward Pass

Scrum
awarDeD

Forming
a scrum

Penalty
kick

Free
kick

ADvantage

Try anD
Penalty try

Knock on

Not releasing Ball
immeDiately in the tackle

Tackler or tackleD
Player not rolling away

# REFEREE'S HAND SIGNALS

Driving to ground
near tackle

Intentionally Collapsing
ruck or maul

Prop Pulling
Opponent Down

Throw in at
scrum not straight

Throw in at
lineout not straight

Forming
a scrum

Obstruction in
general play

High tackle
(foul play)

Dissent (Disputing
referee's Decision)

Ball held up
in-goal

Video
replay

13

# RULES BY AGE GROUP

| Regulation | Leprechaun | Stage 1 | Stage 2 | Stage 3 |
|---|---|---|---|---|
| Age group(s) on 1st Jan | 7's | 8's | 9's & 10's | 11's & 12's |
| Ball size | 3 | 3 | 3 | 4 |
| Time per half – single match (minutes) | 15 | 15 | 15 | 20 |
| Time per half – blitz days (minutes) | 7 | 7 | 7 | 7 |
| No. of minutes allowed on day events | 60 | 70 | 70 | 70 |
| Minimum time allowed for half time | 1 minute | 1 minute | 1 minute | 1 minute |
| Maximum no. of players per team | 8 | 8 | 8 | 10 |
| Number of forwards | N/A | N/A | 3 | 5 |
| Number of backs | N/A | N/A | 5 | 5 |
| Safety zone between pitches (metres) | 6 | 6 | 6 | 6 |
| Tackle height | Touch on Shorts | Waist | Waist | Waist |
| Hand off | No | No | No | Below Shoulder |
| Time allowed for rucks and mauls | N/A | 5 sec | 5 sec | 5 sec |
| No. of players allowed in R/M per side | N/A | 3 | 3 | 5 |
| Kicking allowed | No | No | No | Defence Zone Only |
| Start match | Pass Off | Pass Off | Pass Off | Kick Off |
| Method of scoring | Try | Try | Try | Try |
| Min. No. of players on panel blitz days | No Min | No Min | 12 | 14 |
| Lineout | No | No | 3 Man | 5 Man |
| Scrum | No | No | 3 Man No contest | 5 Man strike and 1 step allowed |
| Pitch Size | 1/4 Pitch | 1/4 Pitch | 1/4 Pitch | 1/2 Pitch |

Due to variations in the physical, mental, social and emotional developments of young children, players under the age of 7 should not be encouraged to play full contact games. Children in this age group should be introduced to Rugby Union through Leprechaun Rugby.

## LEPRECHAUN RUGBY

Leprechaun Rugby has been developed to introduce the Game of Rugby Union to young players new to the Game. The non-tackling and soft-contact nature of Leprechaun Rugby contains all the running and handling skills of Rugby Union. It is a game which is designed to be **FUN**.

### Number of players
Can vary from 4-a-side to 8-a-side and/or 10-a-side games where the emphasis is on the introduction of the skills, inclusion of all participants, safety and enjoyment.

### Playing area
Depends on the number of participants and may vary from 10mx20m to 30mx40m or 50mx70m.

### Duration of games
Depends on the time available and can vary from 5 minutes each way to 10 minutes or 15 minutes each way. Young players (beginners) playing non-contact rugby can only play a maximum 60 minutes of rugby per day.

### Start of play
The game starts by a pass-off with the referee indicating the mark. The opposition must be 5 to 10m away depending on the size of the playing area and the size of the teams.

### Attacking team
The attacking team carries the ball down field, running, passing (or handling) back to score a try by placing the ball over or behind the opposition goal line. The ball can only be transferred to a player behind the ball-carrier. No forward (handling) or passing allowed.

### Defending team
The defending team attempts to halt the running progress of the attacking team by tagging the ball-carrier.

### Tagging
To tag a player the opposition must contact the ball-carrier with two hands (one on each side of the hips). The ball-carrier must then (immediately) pass backwards within a maximum of 3 steps. Any attempt to deliberately gain territory without trying to pass will result in loss of possession, or if the ball-carrier can't see anyone to pass to he/she should (immediately) stop, turn and present the ball immediately to a support player. The support player must then take the ball and pass to another player without running.

### Offside
Applies only to the pass-off and the ball take.

### Gaining possession
The defending team can gain possession as follows: intercepting the ball, gathering a dropped ball, from a knock-on, from a forward pass or a ball in touch.

### Intercepting the ball
An opposition pass can be intercepted.

### Gathering a dropped ball
If the attacking team drops or throws the ball to the ground, the defending team can pick up the ball and play on.

### Knock-on
If the attacking team knocks the ball on (dropping a pass forward) the defending team will restart with a pass-off.

### Forward pass
Forward passes are not allowed and a pass-off is awarded to the non-offending team.

### Ball in touch
If the ball or attacking player carrying the ball crosses or touches the touchline, play is restarted by a pass-off awarded to the non-offending team.

### Penalties
All penalties are taken with a pass-off. A player from the non-offending team taps the ball on the ground with his foot and then passes to a team-mate. Opposing players must be 5 to 10m back depending on the size of the team and/or the pitch.

**Tell the coach if you are not getting enough Ball**

**Reasons for penalties**

1. Ball-carrier hands-off a player.
2. Interference by a defending player not allowing a transfer, pass or ball take immediately after a tag.
3. Ball-carrier makes further ground after a tag without passing, transfer or ball take.
4. A defending player takes the ball from the ball-carrier.
5. Deliberate obstruction of an opponent.
6. A defending player is offside.
7. In all instances the opposition must be 5 to 10m back depending on the size of the teams or the pitch.

## MINI RUGBY

### Start of Match and/or Restarts

*Mini 1 & Mini 2 (8's, 9's & 10's)*

All starts and restarts are by pass-off (from the ground) and must be after the referee's whistle. The opposition must retire 10m from the ball and can only move once the scrumhalf/passer passes the ball. The first receiver must start no more than 2m back from the scrumhalf/passer. At the start of both halves and after a try, the pass-off from the centre of the pitch will be used to restart the game.

*Mini 3 (11's & 12's)*

Starts - Drop Kick on half-way and must be after the referee's whistle. In dead ball situations the restarts must take place 10m from try-line (kicking zone).

*If you Don't understand...Just ask the coach to explain*

### Penalties

### NO QUICK TAP PENALTIES ALLOWED.

*Mini 1 & Mini 2 (8's, 9's & 10's)*

Penalties are taken by a pass-off (from the ground) and after the whistle, the opposition being 10m back from the mark (or behind the goal line). Penalties must be taken through the mark. To play the ball, it must be first tapped with the foot before being passed off the ground. The first receiver must start no more than 2m back from the scrumhalf/passer.

*Mini 3 (11's & 12's)*

Penalties must be taken through the mark designated by the referee. A scrum to be awarded to the opposition if persistently done incorrectly. Opposition must be 10m back or behind the goal line. To play the ball, it must be first tapped with the foot before being passed off the ground. The first receiver must start no more than 2m back from the scrumhalf/passer. Penalties inside the Kicking Zone: The DEFENDING team awarded the penalty may kick directly to touch and are awarded a throw in.

### Hand-off

*Mini 1 & Mini 2 (8's, 9's & 10's)* - Not allowed.
*Mini 3 (11's & 12's)* - Hand-off only allowed below the shoulder.
Penalty awarded if hand-off is to the face or neck.

## Kicking

*Mini 1 & Mini 2 (8's, 9's & 10's) - Not allowed.*

*Mini 3 (11's & 12's)*

It is not permitted to kick the ball outside the 'Kicking Zone' (10m from own goal line). If the offence is unintentional, a scrum is awarded to the opposition and, if intentional, a penalty is awarded to the opposition. Pass back into Kicking Zone rule (as per 15-a-side) to apply. Players in front of the kicker must be brought onside before they can take part in play.

## Lineout

*Mini 2 (9's & 10's)*

(3 players including the Thrower)

1. Lineout 2m from touch line.
2. No contest.
3. Ball must be caught and delivered to scrumhalf, lineout is over when the scrumhalf passes the ball.
4. Both hookers/throwers must be at the front of the lineout and both scrumhalves behind their forwards.
5. Scrumhalves must pass the ball - no break allowed.
6. Both back lines 5m back from lineout.
7. Ball must be thrown straight into the lineout - no over throw.
8. No catch and drive allowed.

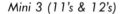

## NO LIFTING ALLOWED IN MINI RUGBY UP TO AGE 16

*Mini 3 (11's & 12's)*

(5 players including the Thrower)

1. Line-out 2m from touch line.
2. The ball may be contested.
3. A space of 1m (arm's length) between all players in the lineout.
4. Both hookers/throwers must be at the front of the lineout and both scrumhalves behind their forwards.
5. Both back lines 5m back from lineout.
6. Ball must be thrown straight into the lineout - no over throw.
7. Lineout is over when the scrumhalf passes the ball/makes a break or when team catching the ball catches and drives (5 seconds 'Use it or Lose it' in driving maul to apply).

## Scrum

*Mini 2: (3 players) (9's & 10's)*

1. All players stay bound until ball has emerged.
2. No push or contesting allowed, ball must be put in straight.
3. Opposition scrumhalf behind his forwards - no follow around allowed.
4. Scrum is over when ball is in the hands of the attacking scrum-half.
5. Scrumhalf must pass the ball – no break allowed.
6. Both back lines 5m back from scrum.
7. Always 10m from touch line and 5m from goal line.

*Mini 3: (5 players) (11's & 12's)*

1. All players stay bound until ball has emerged.
2. Scrum may not move further than 1 step from the mid-point of original scrum.
3. Only hookers can contest strike.
4. Scrumhalf to feed the ball into the scrum with two hands and straight.
5. No forward allowed to pick up the ball from the scrum.
6. Opposition scrumhalf behind his second rows - no follow around allowed.
7. Both back lines 5m back from scrum.
8. Always 10m from touchline and 5m from goal line.
9. Scrum is over when referee calls 'scrum over' or when the ball is in the hands of the scrumhalf, who may break.

**Rules are subject to change in line with Union or Local Branch Guidelines and are correct at time of publishing.**

**Rules & Laws Change – So Keep Up to Date**

## Rucks and mauls

1. Referee/Coach should count down '5,4,3,2,1' from moment ruck/maul is formed. The 'Use it or Lose it' rule should be strictly applied.
2. It is ILLEGAL to COLLAPSE a Maul.
3. Players joining a Ruck or Maul must do so in a safe and legal manner, eg, no shoulder-charging, diving off feet, etc.

People unfamiliar with the game of rugby are often surprised – and always impressed – by how the participants conduct themselves both on and off the pitch. The referee is never abused, the opponent is always applauded.

The key to this is an underlying, solid foundation of mutual respect.

"
**'The Golden Rule' - treat others as you would like to be treated**
"

## To The PLAYERS

1. Always remember, you are out there to have fun.
2. Play within the laws of the game.
3. Keep control, do not lose your temper.
4. Accept the referee's decision; let your captain or coach ask questions.
5. Respect your opponent; never bully or take advantage of a player.
6. Always do your best, and commit to your school or club.
7. Tackle hard but fairly; never attempt to hurt an opponent.
8. Be a good sport, applaud all good play, whether by a team-mate or opponent.
9. You win some, you lose some: be humble when you win, be dignified when you lose.
10. Be part of the team: cooperate with your team-mates, and understand everyone in the squad is important to the team.
11. At the end of a match, thank your opponents and the referee.

## To The COACHES

1. Remember you are in charge of children and teenagers and you have a duty of care to them.
2. Lead by example: be a role model your players can respect.
3. Encourage respect for team-mates, opponents and match officials.
4. Create a safe and enjoyable environment in which to train and play.
5. Ensure your players understand the laws of the game, which only work when everyone agrees to abide by them.
6. Be generous with your praise and easy with your criticism; never shout at a player.
7. Try to ensure everyone gets some game time.
8. Be sure you have the qualifications appropriate to the level you are coaching.
9. Follow professional and medical advice when determining a player's fitness.
10. Help to develop policies for your school/club concerning injury prevention, treatment, discipline, etc.

**To the PARENTS**

1. Remember, your child is playing rugby for their enjoyment, not necessarily for yours.
2. Encourage your child to obey the laws of the game.
3. Teach them that winning isn't the only goal, that honest effort is its own reward.
4. Set a good example by applauding good play on both sides.
5. Never ridicule, embarrass or shout at a player for making a mistake.
6. Do not force a child to play.
7. Never publicly question a referee's judgment or honesty, and recognise their value as volunteers.

> " **Remember that although young people play organised rugby they are not 'miniature internationals'** "

**To the SUPPORTERS**

1. Do not use abusive or foul language towards players, coaches or referees.
2. Respect your team's opponents, and applaud good play by either side.
3. Do not condone violence.

**Referee abuse is unacceptable at any level of Rugby**

**To the REFEREES**

1. Ensure that safety is paramount.
2. Never treat an injury unless qualified to do so.
3. Be punctual, prepared, and well presented.
4. Never criticise individual players, coaches or parents.
5. Maintain the highest standards of personal conduct.
6. Agree times when you may enter a dressing-room and ensure members of the team management are there.
7. Ensure you are a member of a referees' association and have the appropriate qualifications for mini rugby.
8. Respect the rights and dignity of every child; treat everyone equally, regardless of gender, disability, ethnic origin, etc.
9. Be mindful of the boundaries between a working relationship with the players and casual friendship.

In a perfect world, you, as coach, could micro-control every aspect of your players' preparation and training. And in professional rugby, that's what happens. The coaches have virtually full-time access to the players: they are weighed regularly, individually supervised in training, personal diet regimes are drawn up.

Unfortunately, you do not have such luxury. Instead, you are dealing with children and teenagers who are in your charge for only a few hours a week. They might come to training straight from the classroom, or arrive at the club for a match having just finished training for or playing another sport altogether.

So, when it comes to nutrition, the best you can do is to educate your players about eating well, give them the proper guidelines and set a good example yourself.

The secret, as everyone knows, is maintaining a balanced diet. That means getting the right types and amounts of foods and drinks to supply nutrition and energy for maintaining body cells, tissues and organs, and for supporting normal growth and development.

A balanced diet features a variety of foods from the Five Food Groups, for example,

## MILK GROUP (Dairy Products)
- Cheese (fat-free)
- Milk (fat-free or low-fat)
- Yoghurt, regular or frozen

## MEAT AND BEANS GROUP
- Beans, lentils, peas
- Tofu and other soy-protein products
- Beef, pork (select lean cuts, trim away visible fat), poultry with skin removed, fish
- Nuts and seeds (almonds, mixed nuts, peanuts, peanut butter, sunflower seeds)

**Eating your vegetables makes you Big and Strong**

## FRUIT GROUP
- Apples, bananas, berries, grapes, orange, peaches
- Raisins and other unsweetened dried fruits
- 100% fruit juice

## VEGETABLE GROUP
- Potatoes, tomatoes, broccoli, cauliflower, carrots, cucumbers, french beans, spinach
- 100% vegetable juice

## GRAIN GROUP (Bread and Cereals)
- Whole-grain breads, rolls, bagels, cereals (hot and cold)
- Pasta and rice

## OIL
- Low-fat salad dressing
- Low-fat mayonnaise
- Vegetable oil

## HYDRATE WELL
Taking on fluids is as important before training as during the exercise. But don't overdo it. A player should take in no more than 200ml of water, at regular, 15-20 minute intervals.

## PRE-TRAINING SNACK
Ideally, your players should get in some sort of carbohydrate snack about two hours before training. Examples:
- Fresh vegetable soup
- A sandwich on wholemeal bread
- Beans on toast
- Scones
- Breakfast cereals
- Bananas or yoghurt

Only Drink water... Tap or Bottled

## POST-TRAINING POWER SNACK
Recent studies have shown that players who take some protein and carbohydrate immediately after a work-out recover more quickly and can work harder in the next session. Examples:
- A banana and sports drink
- A tuna sandwich
- A bowl of muesli
- Mixed nuts

## Sample Breakfast Menu

Average bowl of Shredded Wheat

Two scones - low fat spread and jam

Two wholemeal toast, low fat spread & jam

Bowl of Cornflakes sweetener/fruit to sweeten

Average bowl of porridge (sweetener optional)

Fruit of your choice with natural low fat yoghurt

Mushrooms on toast

Beans on toast

Scrambled eggs and two turkey rashers

Two scotch pancakes and a banana

Average bowl of Crunchy Nut Cornflakes

Breakfast muffins with scrambled egg

## Sample Lunch Menu

Chicken salad sandwich

Low fat cheese and pickle sandwich

Ham salad sandwich

Egg and salad sandwich (no mayonnaise)

Hummus sandwich (or variation of)

Chicken and noodle soup

Bagel filled with ham and cheese

Spaghetti Hoops on two wholemeal toast

Salad with any meat/fish

Low fat pasta salad

Pitta bread with topping of choice

Soup and two wholemeal bread

## Sample Dinner Menu

Chicken stir fry

Pasta and tomato sauce

Spaghetti bolognese

Mushroom pasta

Jacket potato, with cheese and salad

Tuna salad

Chicken fajitas

Tuna pasta - with tinned tomato and vegetables

Vegetable/meat omelette

Stuffed peppers (with rice or cous cous)

Beef tacos and salad

Lasagne (use low fat sauce and cheese)

Roast meat of your choice (excluding roast potatoes)

Jacket potato with baked beans

Sweet and sour chicken and rice

Chicken caesar salad

Chilli and rice

Beef/chicken casseroles

Chicken/beef curry (not korma)

Chicken in black bean sauce and rice

## Sample Snacks

Apples, grapes,

Bananas, strawberries

Rice cakes

Cereal bars

Low fat yoghurt

Carrot batons/cauliflower/celery with low fat dips

# SUPPLEMENTS and RUGBY

We have all seen how the game of rugby has changed since it became professional almost 20 years ago. In particular, professional players have become physically much bigger, stronger and heavier.

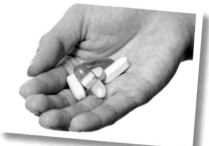

The consequences of this professionalism have trickled down to age grade rugby. Many young players, eager to succeed and to emulate their heroes, believe they must become as big as they can as fast as they can. **And, sadly, some coaches encourage this belief.**

So young players, rather than rely on sound training methods and good nutrition, are tempted to gamble on the "quick fix" solution of taking banned supplements.

But the potential dangers of using such products far outweigh any as yet unproven benefits. Adolescents, in particular, who use muscle-bulking agents are at risk of developing potentially career-ending injuries caused by introducing over-developed muscles onto an immature skeleton. The use of muscle-bulking agents in adolescents is strongly discouraged on health grounds.

**A successful individual performance in rugby is related to a number of factors that include talent, coaching and skill acquisition, structured training and conditioning, motivation, dedication, optimal nutrition, adequate sleep and recovery. None of these can be replaced by the use of sports Supplements.**

**Rugby Unions also have these guidelines:**

1. Young players should focus on good eating and drinking habits to maintain best performance.
2. Coaches, schools, teachers and others involved in training young players should not recommend the use of protein or banned supplements.
3. Rugby Unions strongly advise against the use of ergogenic aids (which enhance energy use, production, or recovery), in particular creatine, by players under 18.
4. Young players with medical conditions - examples, diabetes, asthma, coeliac disease or allergies - should receive appropriate medical and nutritional advice.

Put simply, the risks associated with the use of supplements by young athletes have not been properly studied or assessed.

## CREATINE

For many years, there has been a great deal of anecdotal evidence that the 'supplement of choice' among young rugby players is creatine.

In fact, creatine is already manufactured by the body in the liver, kidneys and pancreas. It also occurs naturally in foods such as meat and fish.

**Don't let Drugs Destroy your future**

Players who take creatine usually do so to improve strength, but the long-term and short-term effects of creatine use by adolescents haven't been studied. Equally, creatine has not been found to increase endurance or improve aerobic performance.

The most common side effects of creatine supplements include weight gain due to fluid retention, diarrhoea, abdominal pain and muscle cramps.

Although it is not illegal in most rugby playing countries, or on the World Anti-Doping Agency list of banned substances, Rugby Unions strongly advise against its use.

> **Creatine or any sport supplement will not replace the size and strength gained from well planned training and recovery, supported by adequate eating and fluid intake.**

## ALCOHOL

It should go without saying that alcohol use has no place in the lives of young players. In the short term, it damages balance, eye-hand coordination and reaction time. It also affects strength, speed and endurance.

**NO ALCOHOL**

It also acts as a diuretic - produces more urine - which can lead to dehydration, and reduces the muscles' ability to replenish glycogen stores. Both mean it takes longer for the body to recover.

## IN CONCLUSION

Sports supplements cannot replace a well-designed programme of training and nutrition in helping to build size, strength and endurance. Also, the unknown long-term effects of their use by adolescents means they simply cannot be recommended to young rugby players.

The mantras have, by now, become clichés: "I just had to stay focused", "I just stayed in the moment", "I just went through my routine", "It's just one match/shot at a time".

But these mantras are everywhere in sport because they have proved to be effective. We understand now that what's going on in a player's head – their mental fitness - is just as important to success and self-fulfilment **(remember, it's not all about winning)** as their basic physical fitness.

And just as physical fitness can be improved through proper exercise, a player's, or a team's, mental fitness can be improved through proper training and repetition.

Much of this involves building self-confidence. You may be the strongest, tallest, most powerful player on the field, but if you aren't confident in your abilities then you'll struggle to reach your goals. Work on improving your confidence just as you work on developing your sport-specific skills. And understand that confidence ebbs and flows, so don't be too hard on yourself when it takes a knock.

Some of the main principles of modern sports psychology are:

1.  **Be Prepared.**
2.  **Stay Focused.**
3.  **Self Talk.**
4.  **Set Goals.**

**Be Positive
Stay Positive**

## 1. BE PREPARED

Although many might think Roy Keane coined the phrase, it was probably Benjamin Franklin who first formulated the idea:

## " Fail to Prepare, Prepare to Fail "

This applies to every aspect of the work you put in: every workout, every training session, every match.

This is as true for coaches as it is for players. Be on time for training, ready to focus solely on the job at hand. Have the right gear. Be clear what you are attempting to achieve or improve upon.

## 2. STAY FOCUSED

As a player, you can control only your own actions, what you are doing — not what anyone else is doing. So stay focused on yourself. If you focus on results — that is, the future, what you can't control — you will simply become frustrated and anxious.

Practice makes Perfect — Practice makes Permanent ...

Focus on the "process", the details of what you are doing. For example, when passing to a team-mate two metres to the left: where are my hands, where am I aiming?

Work on how to stay calm under pressure. For example, take deep breaths, or stretch a bit.

Build a routine that keeps you focused. In rugby, the best goal-kickers, like Johnny Wilkinson and Johnny Sexton, always talk about their "routine". Build one that suits you and stick to it.

Use 'mental imagery', or, in other words, practise seeing yourself perform at your best even before you reach the training ground or ahead of a match. This helps you to relax and, again, focus on what you can control.

## " The best motivation always comes from within "

## 3. SELF-TALK

We all constantly have a little conversation going on in our heads. For the sports person, these can often turn negative: I'm too small, I can't do that.

But you can learn to get rid of negative thoughts.

To begin creating a more positive self-talk, choose one or two mantras to use during training. This could be a simple affirmation, like "I feel strong", or a simple, positive phrase you can repeat over and over, like "Go, Go, Go".

When you have mastered this, and do it almost unconsciously, introduce longer phrases specific to your needs. For example, "I'm a great tackler", or "They won't catch me".

The phrases you choose should let you immediately call up an image of you doing exactly what you say. The image, along with the words, forms a powerful combination to create not only a positive message but also full self-belief.

Share your goals and plans with family and friends to help encourage you. Those closest to you are probably your biggest fans, but may not know that you want or need their encouragement.

Also, a great way to motivate yourself is to provide support to others. Enthusiasm and encouragement can be contagious, and encouraging others to perform to their best often results in them doing the same for you.

> " **Don't carry your mistakes around, place them under your feet and use them as stepping stones to rise above them** "

## 4.  SET GOALS

Giving yourself goals, both short-term and long-term, gives you a purpose and direction and allows you to see incremental success. This increases your confidence. The goals must be realistic and positive. Goals also encourage you to battle on through initial setbacks as you achieve more and more.

One method of setting goals is called 'SMARTER'

**S is for SPECIFIC**
make your goal as precise and detailed as possible, example, I want my box-kick to go exactly 20 metres.

**M is for MEASURABLE**
be able to quantify or rate your current position and then see how much improvement is required. For example, I convert 70% of goal kicks from 30 metres; want to convert 80%.

**A is for ACCEPTED**
goals need to be shared and negotiated with all others involved.

**R is for REALISTIC**
the goal is realistic and positive, yet challenging.

**T is for TIMED**
give yourself a deadline for achieving it.

**E is for EXCITING**
set goals that you truly want to achieve.

**R is for RECORDED**
keep a written record of the goal and the progress made.

Your Best is always Good Enough

At the best of times, getting children to pay attention and making sure your instructions are clear and fully understood is a challenge. But children can't be properly engaged in their training if they don't really understand it, and if they don't understand, there will be no fun. And the younger they are, the more this is true.

## "Communication with your players is paramount"

But what if one of your charges in the Mini Rugby squad has a hidden disability, such as Asperger's Syndrome? In recent years, more and more children are being diagnosed with conditions such as Attention Deficit Disorder (ADD), Attention Deficit Hyperactivity Disorder (ADHD), Oppositional Deficit Disorder (ODD) or Dyspraxia. So it is not unusual now for a coach to be asked to deal with this challenge.

Physically, the child appears just like the others, but he/she may struggle to communicate with and to understand others. They may come across as uninterested, but the opposite may be the case.

### ADAPT

So it is up to the coach to try to understand more about the individuals you are working with, and tailor your coaching and communication skills to address various needs. This will help you to include that player or players as fully as possible within the squad.

So, to start, you must know something about the challenges the children are facing.

### PLAYERS WITH ASPERGER'S SYNDROME:

1. Do not pick up on social cues and may lack inborn social skills, such as being able to read body language, start or maintain a conversation, or take turns talking.
2. Are unable to recognise subtle differences in your tone or accent which change the meaning of your words. So the child may not understand a joke, or may take a sarcastic comment literally. And his or her speech may be flat and hard to understand because it lacks tone, pitch and accent.
3. Have delayed motor development, so may struggle, for instance, to catch a ball.
4. Dislike changes in routine.
5. Appear to lack empathy.

## WHAT ARE ADD & ADHD?

These two are much the same, but with hyperactivity factored in for some children. Players with these conditions may be:

1. Inattentive, but not hyperactive or impulsive.
2. Alternatively, hyperactive and impulsive, but able to pay attention.
3. Most commonly, both inattentive and hyperactive.

## SYMPTOMS OF INATTENTION IN CHILDREN

1. Doesn't pay attention to details.
2. Makes careless mistakes.
3. Appears not to listen when spoken to.
4. Has difficulty remembering things and following instructions.

## SYMPTOMS OF HYPERACTIVITY IN CHILDREN

1. Fidgets with hands or feet.
2. Leaves their place when remaining there is expected.
3. Runs about excessively.
4. Talks excessively.

## SYMPTOMS OF IMPULSIVITY IN CHILDREN

1. Blurts out answers before questions have been completed.
2. Has difficulty waiting their turn.
3. Interrupts or intrudes on others (e.g., Butts into conversations or games).

## WHAT IS OPPOSITIONAL DEFIANT DISORDER (ODD)?

It's not unusual for children to defy authority now and then. They may argue, disobey or talk back to their parents, teachers or other adults. When this behaviour is excessive compared to what is usual for the child's age, it may signal ODD. The child displays a continuing pattern of uncooperative, defiant, hostile and annoying behaviour toward authority figures.

Always know your parents' mobile phone numbers

## SYMPTOMS OF 'ODD' IN CHILDREN

1. Often loses temper.
2. Argues with adults and authority figures.
3. Refuses to comply with adult requests.
4. Blames others for his/her mistakes.
5. Deliberately annoys people.
6. Is easily annoyed by others.
7. Is angry/resentful and spiteful/vindictive.

**If you Don't Pass, you might Become 'Billy No Mates'**

## WHAT IS DYSPRAXIA?

Dyspraxia will present a particular challenge to a sports coach, as the condition relates to difficulty with planning and carrying out sensory or motor tasks. Thus, they can find coping at game time very hard, even distressing. Children with dyspraxia can be of average or above average intelligence but are often behaviourally immature.

## SYMPTOMS OF DYSPRAXIA IN CHILDREN MAY INCLUDE:

1. Poor balance.
2. Difficulty with throwing and catching a ball.
3. Poor awareness of body position in space.
4. Poor sense of direction.

**" When it comes to rugby, every school or club should operate on the principle that there is a place on the pitch for every child "**

## ADAPT AN OPEN DOOR POLICY

One of the glories of sport is that it can embrace everyone, whatever the talent, or whatever the handicap. The incredible feats of the Para-olympians and the beauty of the Special Olympics prove that sport is for all. But for this to work, everyone - coaches, teachers and, importantly, parents - must cooperate to give every child the best chance to participate. Parents should be encouraged to talk with the coaches and school/club officials about any concerns they may have about a child's development, whether physical or emotional. Equally, the parents - and children - must be assured that any discussion is treated in complete confidence and discretion. With everyone's cooperation, every child can have fun playing the game.

# PRINCIPLES FIRST – Ethical Coaching

## COOPERATION

No coach is an island. Often a coach will need help from colleagues in other sports and professions, such as doctors or physiotherapists. Always engage fully and communicate clearly with such professionals to diagnose, treat and manage any player's physical or psychological problems.

> **" Ethical standards comprise such values as integrity, responsibility, competence and confidentiality "**

## INTEGRITY

Do not criticise your fellow coaches in public. Differences of opinion should be dealt with personally and in private. More serious disputes should be referred to the club/school authorities.

## EQUALITY AND DISCRIMINATION

We all deserve to be respected for who we are. In practice, this means a coach must ensure everyone is treated equally while under their watch, regardless of gender, ethnic origin, religion, sexual orientation or political persuasion.

**Cheaters never win ... so always play by the rules**

**One of the great things rugby teaches people is discipline. It's one of the qualities a Coach can instil in players.**

## CONFIDENTIALITY

A delicate subject. Coaches and players must reach some agreement as to what is confidential information. However, this confidentiality does not preclude the disclosure of information to people entitled to know, particularly, for example, in instances of sexual, verbal, physical or emotional abuse.

## ABUSE OF PRIVILEGE

A coach must not attempt to gain personal benefit or reward by exercising undue influence over a player's performance.

## RELATIONSHIPS

A key goal of a healthy Player/Coach relationship is to develop the player's independence. Players must be encouraged to accept responsibility for their behaviour, not just in training or in competition, but also in their social life.

Clearly, a coach should never encourage a player to violate the 'Laws of Rugby' — to cheat — and should deal clearly and fairly with a player who attempts to do so.

Despite modern pressures, a coach must never promote or condone the use of prescribed drugs or banned performance-enhancing substances.

Treat your opponents and the officials with respect, in both victory and defeat, and by that example encourage players to behave likewise.

A coach must accept responsibility for the conduct of the players and discourage inappropriate behaviour.

**Respect your Coaches and your mates**

> **A good Coach will be concerned primarily with the well-being, health and future of the individual player and only secondly with the optimising of performance**

## PERSONAL STANDARDS

You set the example. A coach must always display high personal standards and project a good image of the game and of the job of coaching to players, other coaches, officials and the public.

It goes without saying that a coach should never drink before working in any capacity, and should not smoke when with players. You are responsible for their well-being.

> **Coaches are given a position of trust by parents and players, and are therefore expected to show the highest standards of behaviour while in the company of age-grade players**

For children, a good coach is a fun coach. Give your players a chance to enjoy themselves. Make sure the surroundings and mood are safe, welcoming and encourage mutual respect among the players.

## 'FUN' PRINCIPLES FOR AGE GRADE PLAYERS

### F is for FUN

Children learn quickly when they enjoy what they are doing. Keep them coming back week after week with fun sessions which also include work on technique.

### U is for UNDERSTANDING

Always remember, children are not little adults. Be conscious of their constant development, both physical and mental, such as hormonal changes and emotional and intellectual maturity.

### N is for NURTURING

This is a long process. Although winning is a great experience, there are many other positives to be gained while working with children, and you will lose many players along the way if winning is your only focus. Instead, take a long-term view, and watch the individuals grow over the years rather than over a season.

## HOW TO USE GAMES IN TRAINING

A well-designed training session should allow players to feel they are dealing with match-like scenarios and pressures while practising. Any work on their skills and technique should emulate how those will be used or needed on match day. This will improve their ability to make decisions, and find tactical choices and options in open play. Also, training through games, in the long run, helps a group of players to develop a collective response to decision-making.

Training through games helps young players to develop both a 'games sense' and an understanding of the game of rugby. Games sense is when a player becomes accustomed to the constantly changing circumstances on the pitch: where their team-mates are, the opposition set-up, the measure of the pitch. All of this helps to improve decision-making. Also, a bit of competition adds to the players' enjoyment and increases their motivation to practise.

Part of this entails you taking a step back and letting 'the game be the teacher'. This, in turn, allows you to recognise problems and guide your players on how to find answers to those problems. Of course, training sessions will always involve some drills on technical skills. Together with game simulation, this is known as Whole-Part-Whole training.

**VIRTUAL MATCHES:** the game can become as close to the real thing, replicating the fluid scenarios and unpredictability of competition.

**DECISION-MAKING:** the players always want to get better, and by focusing on particular skills within these games you can ensure that both skills and decision-making will improve. For example, whether to pass or run, tackle or hold.

**COMPLEMENTARY:** you practice defence and attack at the same time.

**SKILLS-BASED:** the focus is on applying core skills in realistic conditions. For example, footwork: whether to beat a player, make a tackle or enter a ruck.

**VARIETY:** a quick game can be used to prepare the players for the full session, to reinforce a skill following a drill, or as a bit of fun to end practice.

**PROBLEM-SOLVING:** the games allow you to identify problems with the players, or to work on tactics ahead of a real match. The players must then solve the problems in a match-like setting.

Pay full attention and listen to your coaches when they are speaking

**PLAYERS FIRST:** the emphasis is less on you coaching and more on them learning. It encourages them to take more responsibility.

**NON-STOP:** games allow for more players to be fully involved and for longer. There is less time spent 'waiting around'.

**FITNESS:** you can sneak in some dreaded fitness work, as the games can work the players hard.

> **" Teaching through games develops and improves a player's skills by using 'play' rather than 'drills' "**

**MOTIVATION:** players want to play, not go through unending drills. This keeps them fresh.

**REPETITION:** by using different games, you can work on one skill over and over, but in a variety of circumstances.

**COMPETITION:** the players still want to 'win', and so will work harder to solve the problems which you set them.

**TEAM-BUILDING:** the games foster team spirit.

# PLAYING the GAME

**Motivation - Imitation - Perfection**
**A typical coaching session should be:**

1. **WHOLE - Game situation -**
   the coach observes, diagnoses and then remedies
2. **PART - Skill learning -**
   coaching to correct and help players succeed
3. **WHOLE - Game situation -**
   to see whether the progress has been made

## TYPES OF GAMES

There are three types of games, each with clearly defined objectives.

**Small Sided -** These apply rugby skills in varying scenarios. There are few players on either side, so play should be fast. The sides should switch from attack to defence regularly, to allow players plenty of chance to be involved in both. The games have rugby elements, but do not have to be purely rugby games.

**Conditioned -** These focus on skills work within the rules of the game. They allow skills to be constantly reworked while avoiding too much repetition. Attack and defence are more defined, resulting in a more rugby-like game.

**Game Situations -** These work on finding rugby answers to rugby problems. The objective is to replicate match-day conditions to allow the players test themselves under pressure. It's as close to a "real" match as you can get in training.

## HOW TO COMMUNICATE WITH YOUR PLAYERS

1. Be Positive: Avoid sarcasm. Criticism should include tips on improvement.
2. Set short-term Goals: These are easier to understand, results can be seen more quickly and they motivate children.
3. Repetition and Recap: Ask your players for their feedback.
4. Don't put on the Pressure: A young player can be as anxious about giving a right answer as they can be upset about giving a wrong answer; it can hold back players.
5. Be Inclusive: Everyone should feel they can be part of the communication process.
6. Bad Language: Never appropriate at any age.
7. Keep it Short: Raise a few points and move on.

## WHEN TO PLAY

You can use the games at almost any time: as a warm-up, to work on an individual skill or a group skill through phases, or to replicate a particular match situation. You can create a game to practise every facet of a match. Alternatively, a game can be used as a reward, as an incentive to get training going, to break up a session or as a way to wind down. Whatever the circumstances, it can be just as hard as a tough conditioning session.

### Why we should start with a Game Situation?

1. That's why they are here, to play.
2. They learn the demands of the game and how to adapt to them.
3. They develop a better understanding of the game and the laws.
4. They learn the complexities of the game bit by bit.

**THE PITCH AND NUMBERS:** The size of the pitch and the number of players involved are limited only by your imagination. The size of the pitch should be appropriate for the skills of your players. Most games will have two sides of equal number, but if you are left with an odd number, give the spare player to the weaker side, or use rolling substitutions.

**EQUIPMENT:** Very little equipment is needed, and the games can be played anywhere, from the local pitch to inside a school/club gym.

## LET THE PLAYERS FIGURE IT OUT

One of the main aims of these games it to encourage players to make decisions in a match-like scenario. Don't be too quick to offer advice; allow the players the time and space to adapt. After all, in a match it will be up to them to react on the spot. With younger players in particular, do not be obsessed with the laws of the game. Initially there might be chaos, but that's how they learn to adapt and influence a game in match-like conditions.

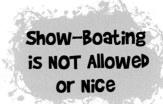

Show–Boating is NOT Allowed or Nice

" **Short group discussions and good questioning can be used to draw out so many different but correct answers** "

# MEASURING SUCCESS

Success is about achieving goals, and winning a match is only one – and often not significant – goal. Instead, get your players to focus on other measures. For example:

1. How many off-loads can we complete?
2. How many turnovers can we make at the rucks?
3. How many times can we cross the gain line?
4. How many times can we make four consecutive passes?

Not only will this keep your players focused on the match, it will also give them a broader perspective. They will think – if we meet our targets, we will probably play well and may even win. If we meet our goals but don't win, we can still leave satisfied with our performance. So too can the coach and the parents. You have often heard a player say, "I really enjoyed that, even if we didn't win". Have fun, come back for more, improve, have more fun.

## How to Measure Success

1. Keeping your players, not just for a season but for 5 to 10 years.
2. New players deciding to join.
3. Building the number of new skills your players can perform, including playing in different positions.
4. Seeing how often those skills are used in matches.
5. Watching how their skill levels progress and their understanding improves.

## DEAL WITH EVERY PLAYER IN THE SAME WAY

No matter how patient you are as a coach, no matter how well-behaved your players are, there will be times when one player, a group or even the squad pushes you to the limit. How you react can have serious and lasting implications. Do not make false threats to players – you were a child once, you know these don't work and will be quickly ignored. Be consistent in how you manage behaviour: do not have one rule for some players and another for the rest. If there's a problem, give the players a chance to explain themselves. Do not accuse them of something without allowing them to defend themselves. If you are in the wrong, admit it and move on. Never engage in discussion with a player in front of the squad, as you may come off the worse. Simply tell the player or players you will discuss it after training. Never swear. The players may find it funny at first, but in time you will lose their respect. And you know well the parents will soon learn of it.

## INTRODUCING CONTACT

Rugby is about contact. The team which dominates contact will almost always dominate possession and control the match. As you move up the age groups, the intensity of the contact in the games will increase. Some children naturally relish contact, many others will be less keen. It is essential your players are introduced to a level of contact appropriate to the age group.

Good technique is crucial to their gaining confidence with the physical aspect of the sport. The training games at the back of this book will fully test your players' skills in contact in a variety of intense, match-like situations. These games will not only develop skills, they are also competitive and motivational. Your players will be keen to put in the effort to win those vital inches.

## " Success is not just about winning "

## FUN COMES FIRST, WINNING A DISTANT SECOND

Children rarely play sport just to win. They play to have fun, to be with their friends, to do something they are good at and to get better at it. But we have all seen too many coaches — and parents — for whom winning is the only thing. So, for the coach, as with the players, fun should be paramount. The sounds of laughter and excited voices, with no fear of failure, are signs of a good training session. There is a perfect circle of development: if your players have fun, they will come back; if they come back for more coaching, they will improve; if they improve, they will come back, and on it goes. Keeping them coming back for more is the true measure of success, not simply winning.

### Why do children play sport?
1. To have fun.
2. To improve their skills.
3. To be with friends.
4. To do something they are good at.
5. For the excitement of competition.
6. To become physically fit.
7. To be part of a team.

As we have emphasised throughout this guide, the main focus for coaches working with age grade players is to ensure the players have fun. One of the duties this entails is ensuring they train and play in a safe environment, e.g. the pitch is in good condition, they wear the proper gear etc.

**Always report inappropriate Behaviour**

But a 'safe environment' does not mean it is only physical injury you must protect your players from; you must also be alert to potential threats of emotional, psychological, and even sexual abuse.

The Government and virtually every large sporting organisation have published detailed guidelines on child welfare, and all are available on-line. Find time to study some of them. Your school or club will also have its own guidelines for you to follow.

But here are some simple rules which will help you, as coach, to protect not only the children in your care, but also yourself.

**"Always have appropriate adult/child ratios"**

**NEVER:**

1. Allow children to use foul language unchallenged.
2. Engage in rough, physical 'horseplay'.
3. Allow, or engage in, inappropriate touching.
4. Share a room with a child alone (if you have an office, keep the door open).
5. Do things of a personal nature which the child can do for themselves.
6. Agree to meet, or travel with, a player on your own.
7. Bring a child to your home.
8. Make even mildly sexually suggestive comments, for example, don't be 'one of the lads' with older players in particular.
9. If possible, avoid taking sessions on your own.

**Never Use Bad Language**

It can be blatant, obvious, or subtle and almost unseen. But it's always nasty and can cause real hurt and injury - physical, emotional and psychological - short term and long term. It can even lead to clinical depression.

And it occurs at every age group, child on child, adult on child - even child on adult.

It is your responsibility as coach both to put an end to it if you see it among your players, and - just as importantly - to ensure it doesn't quietly slip into your own behaviour.

**BULLYING CAN TAKE MANY FORMS, INCLUDING BUT NOT LIMITED TO:**

1. Name calling.
2. Spreading rumours.
3. Excluding others from participating.
4. Isolating others from conversation or play.
5. Threatening and intimidating others.
6. Taking or damaging property or belongings.
7. Actual physical assault and injury.
8. Abusive text messaging or comments on social media.

**Tell the coach if you see or are being bullied**

From the coach's perspective, a child - or group of children - can attempt to bully you through intimidating or threatening gestures and comments.

Equally, a coach must ensure 'constructive criticism' doesn't slide into behaviour which humiliates or degrades a child or group.

**DEALING WITH BULLYING**

Every school or club should have a clear, publicised and regularly reviewed policy on how to deal with incidents.

More extreme examples of bullying should be reported to the State health authorities or the police.

A coach must work to ensure everyone is working in an environment where:
1. Name calling is not tolerated.
2. No one suffers any type of abuse.
3. No one is victimised.
4. Everyone is heard and supported.
5. Everyone is treated equally.
6. Problems are solved together.

# REST and RECOVERY

It might not seem obvious, but one of the duties of a good coach is to ensure your players do not over-train. Yes, you want your players to reach their full potential, but you must also be on the look-out for signs that a player is close to going "over the edge".

The player must be both physically and mentally able to cope with the workload of increased training. Research has identified a clear link between training and associated stress on the body's immune system, leading to injury and illness.

## "There is a thin line between training and over-training"

Again, while it may seem obvious, two of the main ingredients of proper recovery are a good night's sleep and a proper diet. As a coach you can have little input into how your young players manage their sleep and what they eat. But you can emphasise the importance of each to them.

Even younger players will realise that the harder they train, the more sleep their body will demand. Training tears down the muscles and these have to be rebuilt. This is best done at night when they are completely at rest.

And proper nutrition is vital. When muscles are broken down in training, those muscles need adequate nutrition to rebuild. A player who skimps on this will quickly feel it.

Tell your players: they don't get strong doing a workout, they get strong only when they recover from the workout.

## Symptoms of Over-Training

| Physiological | Psychological |
|---|---|
| • Increased muscle tenderness | • Disturbed sleep |
| • Lower anaerobic threshold | • Irritability |
| • More susceptibility to illness | • Greater fatigue |
| • Poor appetite | • Depressed mood |
| • Less energy | • Listlessness |
| • Unable to work fully | • Oversensitivity to criticism |

### MONITORING RECOVERY

To get the most out of training, keep a record of certain conditions. For example:
1. **Feeling** - How does the player feel after training?
2. **Mood** - What is their mood like?
3. **Sleep** - Did they get a good night's sleep?
4. **Weight** - Any signs of losing or gaining weight?
5. **Muscle soreness** - Have they any muscle soreness?

## PCERT SCALE FOR CHILDREN

PCERT (Pictorial Children's Effort Rating Table) or RPE which stands for Relative Perceived Exertion. This means 'How hard do I feel I am exercising'. It is a tool you use to tell others how your body is feeling when you exercise. Children who exercise in the numbers 4-7 are getting moderate to vigorous exercise. That means the player's body is getting the right amount to be healthy. Never push your players to the point where they are exercising outside the capacity of their body or age. Please remember that children develop at different stages and are not all capable of the same training programme.

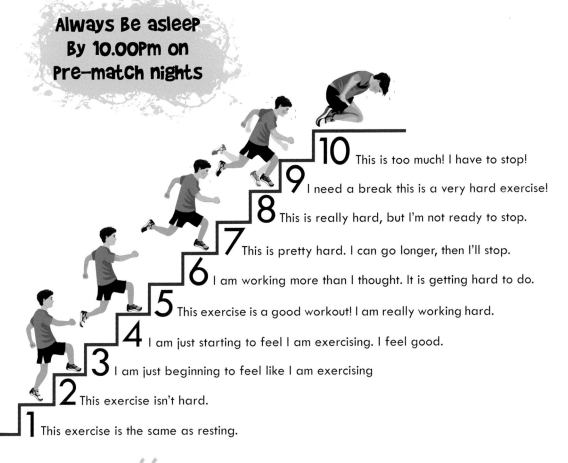

**Always Be asleep By 10.00Pm on Pre-match nights**

10 This is too much! I have to stop!

9 I need a break this is a very hard exercise!

8 This is really hard, but I'm not ready to stop.

7 This is pretty hard. I can go longer, then I'll stop.

6 I am working more than I thought. It is getting hard to do.

5 This exercise is a good workout! I am really working hard.

4 I am just starting to feel I am exercising. I feel good.

3 I am just beginning to feel like I am exercising

2 This exercise isn't hard.

1 This exercise is the same as resting.

**"Try and fail, but never fail to try"**

# ANIMAL WALKS

Whatever the sport, the youngest players — children between 6 to 10 years - need to work on the most basic skills of movement. This is called Locomotor Movement: literally, moving from one spot to another. (Non-locomotor movement is done from a fixed spot.)

As ever, the emphasis is on fun, so as an extended part of the warm-up of a coaching session for the younger age groups we recommend Animal Walks. They are, simply, the children's introduction to strength and conditioning.

only 1 hour
a Day on your
Games console

These walks are designed to improve seven aspects of the child's development:

1. Balance.
2. Cardiovascular endurance - the ability of the heart and lungs to supply fuel during sustained physical activity.
3. Flexibility - the range of motion around a joint.
4. Muscular strength - the ability to exert force.
5. Muscular endurance - the ability of the muscle to continue work without tiring.
6. Speed.
7. Body composition - the relative amount of bone, muscle, fat, etc.

## The Animal Movements

| | | |
|---|---|---|
| Kangaroo Jumps | Dear Leaps | Monkey Walk |
| Flamingo Hops | Crab Walk | Bear Crawl |
| Galloping | Limping Lamb | Caterpillar Walk |
| Mighty Albatross | Gorilla Walk | Alligator Walk |
| Skipping | Frog Walk | Snake Crawl |

## THE BENEFITS OF ANIMAL WALKS

1. Better fitness.
2. Better locomotor skills.
3. They are fun, and so encourage children to continue with physical activity.
4. Increase self-esteem and self-efficiency.
5. Improve general athleticism and body awareness.
6. Fewer accidents/injuries.
7. Help develop the neuromuscular system.

1. Bear Crawl

2. Crab Walk

3. Leap Frog

4. Gorilla Walk

5. Limping Lamb

Try Walking, Cycling or Running to School

Also try ... Horse Galloping, Carioca's Or make them up...

7. Snake Crawl

6. Mighty Albatross

# THE COACHING LADDER

## Age 6–12

# THE COACHING LADDER – Level 1

There are generally 5 recognised levels of coaching progression which coincide with age:

**LEVEL 1** – Step 1, age 6 to 8;  Step 2, age 9 to 10;  Step 3, age 11 to 12.
**LEVEL 2** – Step 4, age 13 to 14.
**LEVEL 3** – Step 5, age 15 to 16.
**LEVEL 4** – Step 6, age 18 to 20.
**LEVEL 5** – Step 7, over 21 to Senior.

For this guide, we focus on the first three levels, which address how a coach interacts with a squad of players from the age of six up to under 16 level. In the modern game, it is highly unlikely anyone with little experience would be working with older players. However, the training exercises at the back of the book are appropriate for even the most senior level of the game.

Note: Different Rugby Unions have extensive and detailed regulations regarding the playing of Mini Rugby, from the size of the ball to the length of a match, from the numbers in a lineout to the type of tackle permitted. They are usually available from Rugby Union websites

## MINI RUGBY

As we have emphasised throughout this guide, the focus for successful nurturing of young players must be on fun. This is never more true than at this level. A coach is dealing with children, boys and girls – and, in truth, may at times feel more like a child minder than a rugby coach.

Nevertheless, some of the most simple concepts and principles of the game can be introduced early on. The children can learn about attack and defence, that the ball can be passed only backward, and they can – mainly through play, rather than through formal training and exercises – begin to develop handling and running skills.

While the "rugby" which the youngest play may quickly deteriorate into everyone screaming and running about the place, through repetition they will begin to understand the game's simple structure.  It is the coach's duty to ensure the players are working in a safe and enjoyable environment. Any advice or corrections offered should be quite general and couched in approval and encouragement, without going into detail. And everyone gets to play and to have fun.

The aim of the coach is to gently guide the young players towards achieving certain development goals and targets.

**Age 6–8**

COACH GUIDES · PLAYER PLAYS · FUN · GAME

## TASKS AND MILESTONES

(In small-sided games, up to eight-a-side)

### TECHNICAL SKILLS

**Handling** (using a size 3 ball)
1. How to throw a ball off the left and right hand.
2. How to catch with hands out and fingers spread.
3. Running and picking the ball off the ground.
4. Running and placing the ball on the ground.
5. The 'Lateral pass' (passing the ball sideways, not forward.

**Running**
1. How to quickly change pace, stop/start to evade opponents.
2. Zigzag running and stepping off the left and right foot.

**Contact** (Tackle below the waist)
1. Get players comfortable with the physical aspect of the sport.
2. Create situations for simple, safe, modified tackling.
3. Work with 'flag' rugby, tip and tag.

**Backline attack** (all play begins with tip and go)
1. Alignment and where to stand to receive a pass.
2. Running with the ball and passing to left and right.

### TACTICAL SKILLS

Introduce the laws of the game, for example:
1. Pass backwards only.
2. Offside.
3. Fair tackle.

**Note:** In all Mini Rugby, the 5 second 'Use it or Lose it' rule applies.
This starts from the moment a ruck/maul is formed.
It is illegal to collapse a maul.

**Always Drink a glass of Water with your meals**

## MENTAL TARGETS

1. Encourage 'Go Forward' rugby - running and evasion in attack.
2. Pass backwards to keep attack moving.
3. Assist team-mates to get the ball back when defending.
4. Emphasise 'fair play' and 'friendly competition'.

Age 6-8

## FOCUS ON THE BROADEST PHYSICAL SKILLS FOR 6-8 YEAR OLDS

1. **BALANCE**
2. **CO-ORDINATION**
3. **MANIPULATION**
4. **LOCOMOTION**
5. **AWARENESS OF BODY IN SPACE**

**Balance:** The ability to control the limbs and whole body in both static and dynamic positions by co-ordinating the eyes, ears and sense of touch - including impulses coming from within the joints. It means activating and controlling key muscle groups to maintain stable joint positions.

*Static Balance* - The ability to keep the centre of mass above the base of support.

*Dynamic Balance* - Maintaining balance while the body is moving.

**Co-ordination:** The ability to control the movement of the body with the senses, e.g, Catching a ball through hand-eye co-ordination.

**Manipulation:** The ability to control a ball or other object or resistance, such as an opponent.

**Locomotion:** The ability to move efficiently while changing speed or type of movement, for example, walk, jog, accelerate, decelerate, jump, spin, bend, stop.

**Awareness:** The ability to control body position, movement and play within the confines of the area.

Many of the exercises, drills and games at this stage will demand that one, some, or all of the above abilities are involved. For example, to complete a fall to the ground a player may engage a combination of balance, locomotion, strength and co-ordination.

The Window for Speed Development is NOW

**Age 9–10**

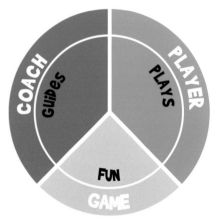

COACH *Guides* · PLAYER *Plays* · FUN · GAME

## TASKS AND MILESTONES
(up to 10-a-side at 10 years)

### TECHNICAL SKILLS

**Handling** (Size 4 ball at 10 years)
1. Pick from the ground and pass off the left and right.
2. Sweep the ball off the ground and pass off the left and right.
3. Start lateral passing, and introduce 2v1 and 3v2 situations.

**Running**
1. Introduce the 'Side Step'.

**Contact** (Tackle below the waist)
1. How to tackle from the side.
2. How to tackle from the front, and where to place the head.
3. How to fall to the ground and place the ball for a team-mate.
4. Practice getting back up quickly to re-join the game.

**Scrummaging** (3 players, uncontested at 8 years; 5 players, strike allowed at 10 years)
1. Introduce the individual body positions in the scrum.
2. Where to bind and place the arms and feet for engagement.
3. How to feed the ball into the scrum.
4. How to 'Strike the Ball'.
5. Most importantly, how to scrum safely.

**Lineout** (3 players at 8 years; 5 players at 10 years; no lifting)
1. How to throw a ball in accurately.
2. How best to jump and catch.
3. How to get the ball to the scrumhalf.

**Maul** (5 second rule)
1. Where the ball-carrier should be and how to remain stable.
2. How to hold the ball to present it securely.
3. The body positions of link players and how to move the ball on.
4. How support players effectively bind and protect the ball.

**NO gum shield, NO TEETH**

**Ruck** (5 second rule)
1.  How the ball-carrier should present the ball.
2.  How the link player should get body position to protect the ball.
3.  How support players effectively bind and protect the ball.

Age
9–10

**Backline attack**
1.  How to re-align as play develops.
2.  How to run to support a team-mate.

## TACTICAL SKILLS
Focus on Mini rugby laws for:
1.  Lineout, scrum, ruck, maul and Advantage.
2.  Instil the importance of honesty and responsibility.

## MENTAL TARGETS
1.  Teach the players the importance of possession - having the ball.
2.  Explain what continuity means - keeping the ball.

## FOCUS ON THE BROADEST PHYSICAL SKILLS FOR 9-10 YEAR OLDS
*As well as consolidating work on:*
1.  Balance
2.  Co-ordination
3.  Manipulation
4.  Locomotion
5.  Awareness of body in space
*Improve on*
6.  **SPEED**
7.  **AGILITY**

**Speed:** The ability to accelerate and move all or part of the body quickly.

**Agility:** The ability to change direction efficiently and effectively.

Again, the central aim is to challenge players with movement tasks so that they may improve while also having fun. Many of these tasks can be used in the warm-up and during breaks in the session. They can also be made into a fun circuit.

# STEP 3 COACHING

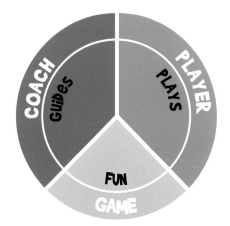

## TASKS AND MILESTONES
(up to 10-a-side)

### TECHNICAL SKILLS

1. Handling (Size 4 ball).
2. Introduce the switch move.
3. Introduce the loop.
4. Learn how making the right decision can create space.

**Running**
1. How to hand-off (below the shoulder).

**Contact**
1. How to tackle from behind.
2. How to pass out of the tackle, with the hands free.
3. How to gain possession while making a tackle.

**Maul**
4. How to bend, bind and drive.

**Ruck**
1. Learn the importance of the ball-carrier placing the ball properly.
2. How support players should bend, bind and drive over the ball.

**Scrum** (5 players)
1. Learn the individual stable body positions.
2. Develop the co-ordination of the scrum as a unit.
3. Explain the safety precautions when dealing with a collapsed scrum.

**Lineout** (5 players)
1. How the catcher and support players turn a lineout into a maul.

**Backline attack**
1. Practice how to see space and attack it.
2. Introduce different patterns of attack.

**Kicking and catching**

Work on all the tactical variations, for example:

1. Grubber kick.
2. Chip kick.
3. Punt.
4. Fielding the ball in the air.

Age
11–12

## TACTICAL SKILLS

1. Go into more detail on the laws of the tackle.
2. Emphasise the importance of how to conduct themselves.

## MENTAL TARGETS

1. Work on defensive techniques designed to win back the ball.
2. Focus on how to play as a team, as a collective, in attack and defence.

## FOCUS ON THE BROADEST PHYSICAL SKILLS FOR 11-12 YEAR OLDS

*As well as consolidating work on*

1. Balance
2. Co-ordination
3. Manipulation
4. Locomotion
5. Awareness of body in space
6. Speed
7. Agility

*Introduce*

8. **TRIPLE EXTENSION**
9. **COOL-DOWN**

Always Play
With Pride and
give it
your Best

**Triple Extension:** The ability to extend at ankle, knee and hip simultaneously (such as during a standing long jump or a vertical jump).

**Cool-Down:** Physical activity which is a slow jog and static stretching after training or a match designed to return the body to its normal functioning.

PASSPORT TO RUGBY

2

# THE COACHING LADDER – Level 2

## Teenagers

Right, coach. Now you're dealing with teenagers – with all the benefits and (certain) drawbacks that entails. Up to now your role has largely been that of a guide, gently encouraging the players to explore and to have fun.

Now, as your players are maturing, your role becomes more that of an instructor. Your players will be undergoing dramatic and rapid development, physically, intellectually and emotionally. They will be eager to learn and to experiment – and will be keen to have their own input into their development.

Often your work will include explaining "why", allowing the players to critically analyse what they are trying to achieve. While you continue to work on their technical and tactical skills for the game, you will also develop a much more structured game.

Be aware your players will respond much more readily to encouragement than to outright criticism, so emphasise the positive.

You are now playing the full 15-a-side game, complete with set-pieces and full tackle. It is your responsibility to ensure it is played in a safe environment.

And remember, as ever, the focus must still be on enjoyment, on fun, with plenty of running and passing, and everyone involved.

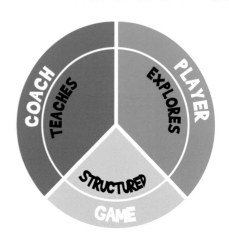

## TASKS AND MILESTONES

### TECHNICAL SKILLS

**Handling - maintain continuity of attack**
1. Teach them where to throw and how to catch.
2. How to 'Spin Pass'.
3. Making the right decision to preserve space.
4. Making the right decision to create space.
5. Guide them through lateral passing and receiving the pass.
6. Drills to perfect the pick and placing of the ball.

**Running**
1. Work on change of pace in a 1v1 situation.
2. How to 'Side Step' an opponent.
3. Introduce the swerve movement.
4. Develop the art of the hand-off.

**Contact – Defence**
1. How to gain possession in the tackle.
2. Develop the front, side and rear tackle.

**Contact – Attack**
1. How to place the ball in the tackle.
2. How to pass around the tackle, by keeping the arms free.
3. Perfect the passing out of the tackle.

**Maul - Maintain continuity in a 'standing' tackle**
1. Show how a ball-carrier should establish a strong base and protect the ball.
2. Explain how link players can secure possession and deliver the ball.
3. Develop how support players should bend, bind and drive.

**Ruck - Recycle quick possession in the tackle**
1. Emphasise to the ball-barrier the importance of ball presentation.
2. Show how support players should protect the ball-carrier and secure ball.

### Ruck - Creating a Ruck to maintain continuity

1. Get the ball-carrier to go to ground and place ball while driving.
2. Show how support players should protect the ball-carrier and secure Ball.

Age
13–14

### Scrum - Attack (8 players, introduction of Backrow)

1. How to form a full scrum with possession.
2. How to engage.
3. Guide the scrumhalf on how to 'Put-in' for the strike on the ball.
4. Explain what channels are - channel 1 and 2.
5. Work on delivery and the use of the ball.

### Scrum - Defence

1. How to form a full scrum without possession.
2. How to engage in defence.
3. Work on contesting possession.

### Lineout - Attack (8 players)

1. How to form a full lineout with possession.
2. Introduce calls and communication and variations.
3. Work on movement and reactions.
4. How to throw, jump, catch and bind.
5. How to deliver and use the ball.

### Lineout - Defence

1. How to form a full lineout without possession.
2. Work on movement and reactions.
3. Work on contesting possession.
4. How to prevent territory being gained.

### Backline Attack - from Scrum, Lineout and Phase play

1. Work on positioning and alignment to allow range of options.
2. How to identify space - recognise a pattern of play.
3. Angles of run - to preserve/create space.
4. Timing of the pass - to hold defenders.
5. Breaking the gainline - with an unmarked player.
6. Support the ball-carrier - to continue attack.

### Backline Attack

1. Work on contesting possession.
2. Display how to prevent territory being gained.

# STEP 4 COACHING – Continued

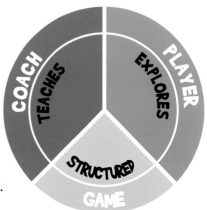

**Kicking and Catching - to exploit space**
1. Develop the grubber and chip in a 1v1 situation.
2. Work on when to punt - essentially to gain ground.
3. How to gain/regain possession when fielding the Ball.

**Defence**
1. Work on their alignment with one another.
2. Maintain alignment when moving forward.
3. Work on recognising a threat and reacting with flexibility.
4. Emphasise the importance of the first-up tackle to prevent loss of territory.

**Restarts - To gain/regain Possession**
**Receiving team**
1. Work on the formation to regain possession.
2. How to protect and deliver the ball from restarts.

**Kicking Team**
1. Where to drop-kick a restart.
2. Move forward in a ppattern to apply pressure.
3. How to contest possession from a restart.

**Eat Well an Hour Before Training or a Match**

## TACTICAL SKILLS
1. Emphasise the importance of their personal behaviour and actions.
2. Carefully study the basic Laws of the 15-a-side game.
3. Be tactically aware of the opposition.
4. Identify with a positional role and how it should be played.

## MENTAL TARGETS
1. Insist on 'Go Forward' rugby and include basic kicking strategies.
2. Support team-mates to maintain continuity in attack.
3. Adopt a collective attitude of team play in attack and defence.

**FOCUS ON THE BROADEST PHYSICAL SKILLS FOR 13-14 YEAR OLDS**

*As well as*

1. Balance
2. Co-ordination
3. Manipulation
4. Locomotion
5. Awareness of body in Space
6. Speed
7. Agility
8. Triple extension introduction
9. Cool-down

Age 13–14

*Concentrate on:*

10. **STRENGTH (including triple extension)**
11. **FLEXIBILITY**
12. **MOBILITY**

This stage of development will take a more formal approach to advance the core and strength capacities of the player. The use of swiss-balls and med-balls will be a feature of both core development and dynamic stability and strength. Players should be introduced to the formal weight lifting techniques of the 'Squat, Clean and Snatch', but strictly without the use of weights and only with the use of a broom handle.

**Strength:** The ability of a muscle(s) to exert force.

**Flexibility:** The range of movement possible both actively and statically about a joint.

**Mobility:** The dynamic range of movement about a joint.

*Also work on:*

1. **Evasion**     -     Speed work in and out through Poles.
2. **Footwork**    -     Ladder work for efficiency and accuracy.
3. **Passing**     -     Various lengths, off both left and right hand.
4. **Rucking**     -     Technique and execution.

This stage assumes that the player is entering secondary school and the physical capacities that are outlined are classified according to secondary school years.

Sample exercises and drills for 13-14 year olds can be covered during warm-ups, circuit training units and in the conditioning section of practice. Some will be more suitable to an indoor setting and will require specialist equipment, for example swiss-balls, Med-balls and gym mats.

PASSPORT TO RUGBY

## THE COACHING LADDER

Age 15–16

3

# THE COACHING LADDER – Level 3

## Maturing Adolescents

Up to now your role as coach has been to act as an instructor. Now the focus turns to that of a mentor who challenges.

Your charges are maturing rapidly, becoming young adults (indeed, the oldest ones will soon be driving). They are highly competitive individually, but they also have a greater awareness of the team, of the collective effort. While they want to be given their freedom, equally they are desperate to be trusted with responsibility, both individually and collectively.

Your task is to challenge them to become more skilled and proficient and achieve higher levels of performance.

Training sessions and matches will be much more competitive. But remember, they must still also be enjoyable, and everyone takes part.

And, as the general intensity has ramped up a gear, so too has your responsibility to ensure everything is conducted in a SAFE environment. As the hits get harder, the injuries get more frequent and more serious. It is your job to ensure they are kept to the minimum.

More emphasis must be put on proper warm-ups and warm-downs.

You will also need to try, as best you can, to monitor your players' "off-site" development, for example their diet (supplements are not recommended), or their weight training regime. You must set an example and educate them on best practice.

The development of the game focuses on working in units, in terms both of players and of tactics, to improve overall performance.

Age
15–16

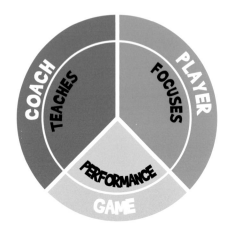

COACH TEACHES
PLAYER FOCUSES
PERFORMANCE
GAME

## TASKS AND MILESTONES

### TECHNICAL SKILLS

**Handling - Learning to beat Defenders**

*Continue working on:*
1. Where to throw and how to catch.
2. Lateral passing and receiving the pass.
3. Deciding when to preserve space.
4. Deciding how to create space.
5. Spin pass.

**Running**

*Continue working on:*
1. Change of pace.
2. How to 'Side Step' an opponent.
3. The swerve movement.
4. The art of the hand-off.

**Contact - Defence**
1. Gaining possession in the tackle.
2. Develop the front, side and rear tackle.

**Contact - Attack**
1. How to place the ball in the tackle.
2. How to pass around the tackle, keeping arms free.
3. Work on passing out of the tackle.
4. Introduce 'Pick-and-Go' from the ruck.

**Maul - Developing an attacking platform**
1. Show how a ball-carrier should establish a strong base and protect the ball.
2. How link players can secure possession and choose best option to deliver the ball.
3. Develop how support players join the link.

Your Best
is always
good enough

### Ruck - Recycling possession after the tackle
1. Work on how ball-carrier presents the ball.
2. Support players both protect ball-carrier and secure the ball.

### Ruck - Creating a ruck to maintain attack
1. Ball-carrier goes to ground under control and places the ball .
2. Support players protect ball-carrier and ball, and assess next move.

### General Support Play
1. Learning to anticipate how play may develop.
2. Running the right lines.
3. Taking up the right position.
4. Working on close support and wide wupport.

### Scrum - Attack
*Continue working on:*
1. Formation.
2. How to engage.
3. Learn to apply pressure.
4. Guide the scrumhalf on how to 'Put-in' for the strike on the ball.
5. Delivery and the use of the ball.

### Scrum - Defence
*Continue working on:*
1. Formation without possession.
2. How to engage in defence.
3. Contesting possession.

### Lineout - Developing a platform for Attack
*Continue working on:*
1. Formation with possession.
2. Varying calls.
3. Movement and reaction.
4. How to throw, jump, catch and bind.
5. How to deliver and use the ball.

### Lineout - Defence
*Continue working on:*
1. Formation without possession.
2. Contesting possession.
3. How to prevent territory being gained.

Age
15-16

**Age 15–16**

### Backline attack - Building Multiple Phases
1. How to see space open as a pattern develops.
2. How to run angles which maintain or create space.
3. How to time a pass to hold a defender.
4. Support the ball-carrier so they are not isolated.
5. Recognise individual roles to allow a pattern to develop.
7. How to choose positions and alignment which allow for options.

### Kicking and Catching - to Exploit Space
1. Practice the chip and grubber kicks in a match scenario.
2. Practice long punt, to touch or behind defence.
3. Practice fielding high kicks.

### Defence - Stopping a line-break and Regaining Possession
1. How to move forward and maintain alignment as a group.
2. Work on reading potential threats and reacting.
3. Practice tackling.
4. Work on supporting the tackler.

### Restarts - Gaining Possession

### Receiving Team
1. Work on positioning.
2. Catching or deflecting the ball.
3. How to deliver the ball.
4. How to initiate an attack.

### Kicking Team
1. Practice the 'Drop-kick'.
2. Learn to move forward in a pattern.
3. Practice challenging for the high ball.

## TACTICAL SKILLS

1. Focus on the precise sanctions attached to infringements of the laws.
2. Concentrate on set-piece play.
3. Develop clear game plans.
4. Focus on attack, seeing and developing space.
5. Emphasise that the players are responsible for their actions and the consequences.

Age
15–16

## MENTAL TARGETS

1. Emphasise principles of play which maintain pressure on opponents.

## FOCUS ON THE BROADEST PHYSICAL SKILLS FOR 13-14 YEAR OLDS

*As well as*

1. Balance
2. Co-ordination
3. Manipulation
4. Locomotion
5. Awareness of body in Space
6. Speed
7. Agility
8. Triple extension introduction
9. Cool-down
10. Strength (including triple extension)
11. Flexibility
12. Mobility

*Concentrate on:*

**13. POWER**

**14 MULTI-ACTIVITY ENDURANCE**

**15 REHABILITATION**

**Power:** The ability to produce strength at speed.

**Multi-activity endurance:** The ability to maintain a high intensity during patterns of movement which mimic match conditions.

**Rehabilitation:** Long-term exercises designed to strengthen the body's core and help to prevent injury.

# The WARM-UP

## GUIDELINES TO WARMING UP

Warming up is an essential part of any exercise. It raises the body temperature and muscle temperature, and prepares the heart, lungs, muscles and nerves for more strenuous physical activity. It is particularly important for avoiding injury. There are four principal warm-up activities, each as important as the others, so do not neglect any of them.

**Always arrive to Training and Matches on Time**

## WARMING UP ACTIVITIES

1. **The General Warm-up**
   This should consist of five minutes of light activity, such as jogging, zigzagging, or jogging backwards and sideways.

2. **Dynamic Stretching**
   These are controlled, soft bounce or swinging motions which gently force a part of the body past its usual range of movement. They can include neck rotation, side bends, hip circles, leg lifts, arm swings or walking lunges, each stretch held for 6-10 seconds.

3. **Rugby-specific Warm-up**
   These focus on movements required for the sport. Activities would include handling drills, running lines and decision-making drills.

4. **Match-specific Warm-up**
   Finally, finish with a series of drills or formations prepared for the match. This should have the players at their physical and mental peak.

> " If you haven't exercised in a while, you may need to Stretch and warm-up before you stretch and warm-up "

For all teams under the ages of 12 years looking simply to warm up, a minimum of 15 minutes should be enough. For rugby at higher grades, you will need to complete a warm-up that could last 30-40 minutes.

**GENERAL RUGBY WARM-UP**

1.  2-3 slow laps of the pitch, including running sideways and backwards, high knees and kicking the heels back.
2.  3 minutes of flexibility stretching, including leg lifts, walking lunges, hamstring walks, torso turns.
3.  5 x 20m runs, from 50% sprint to 80%, and 5 zigzag runs at 80% sprint.
4.  3 minutes of dynamic stretching, including rotating arms, pick left and right, and jump-to-catch.
5.  Rugby-specific drills (handling, running lines), building up to full pace.
6.  Match-specific drills (lineouts, rucks, back-line drills, set-pieces).

Total time: 15-20 minutes.

**DYNAMIC STRETCHING**

WALKING HAMSTRINGS

WALKING SUMOS

WALKING LUNGES

WALKING KNEE LiftS

**MATCH SPECIFIC WARM-UP**

Get your team prepared both mentally and physically for their match.

A pre-match warm-up prepares the body by increasing the blood flow, lung function, heats the body and gets the muscle groups fired up for intense activity. It is also a time for players to focus the mind and carry out some key skills, tactics and team plays.

**HOW LONG**

The warm-up will vary depending on age and also on the weather conditions. On a cold day the body may take longer to reach match readiness while a very warm day may require a less vigorous workout. All aspects should still be covered over 35-50 minutes and the start time for preparation should be worked back from the kick-off time. This is an outline of how you might prepare your team for action.

**PLAYER TIME** : 8-10 minutes

Give your players time to do their own personal stretching and to loosen up by jogging around. Place-kickers, scrumhalves and hookers may want to practise their specific skill while a game of tip rugby may also be a preferred option. This is also a good time for the squad to familiarise themselves with the pitch and its surroundings.

**SQUAD TIME** : 8-12 minutes

Carry out some simple handling drills with an emphasis on communication and eliminating mistakes, like dropped balls. Increase the noise level as well as the complexity of the moves to focus the squad.

### UNIT TIME : 8-12 minutes

Divide the squad into forwards and backs. The backs can run through different moves depending on pitch position while decision-making can be tested in a 3 v 2 situation. Forwards can go through variations of the lineout and set-pieces including scrums.

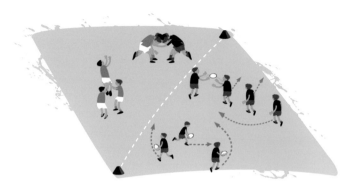

### TEAM TIME : 8-10 minutes

Get the backs to run moves against the forwards by running some attacking plays, both touch tackle and full contact. This should be done either unopposed or against ruck-pad holders, leaving the ball to create phase after phase situations. The use of substitutes can be helpful during this time.

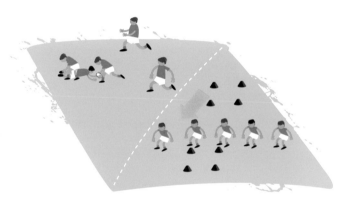

### CONTACT TIME : 5-8 minutes

Finally to prepare the team and to fire them up, get some ruck-pad holders and operate at match pace. Increase the intensity as well as the noise level. Make sure you have water breaks during the warm-up and head back to the dressing room for some final words.

## GUIDELINES TO COOLING DOWN

Every training session or match-day routine should finish with the cool down. If the warm-up aims to increase the heart rate and warm the muscles, the cool down gradually decreases the heart rate and relaxes the muscles and restores the body to its original state.

Gentle cardiovascular exercise, such as jogging or walking, will gradually bring the body temperature down and decrease the heart rate, while stretching will steadily relax the muscles.

The cool down also helps the body dispose of waste products and toxins generated during exercise. The most well known waste product is lactic acid; if this is allowed to build up, it may cause stiffness and cramp the following day.

An effective cool down will also help to prevent dizziness, which can be caused by stopping an activity suddenly, as blood that should be going to the brain is pooled in the extremities. The cool-down stretches also increase flexibility, and might help to prevent DOMS (Delayed Onset Muscle Soreness) - that feeling you can get up to two days after training.

The cool down is as instrumental to the prevention of injury as the warm-up.

## COOL DOWN ACTIVITIES

1.  **Light Jog** - About 3 minutes should do it.

2.  **Stretch** - After training the muscles are warmed up and so are more elastic and pliable. This is when we see the greatest improvement in flexibility. Although stretching hasn't been found to reduce injuries, it does reduce next-day soreness in hamstrings, quads and calves. Depending on the level of your team, stretching should take five to 10 minutes.

3.  **Hydrate** - It is essential to replenish the water the body has used up to help decrease muscle soreness and increase strength and flexibility.

4.  **Nutrients** - As with water, the body needs to replenish the nutrients, such as protein, used during exercise. For players under 18, this could simply be a glass of chocolate milk. Senior players will want to emulate their idols and down a protein shake. These do aid recovery and muscle repair, but be careful in choosing a product, see Supplements and Rugby for further information.

5.  **Cold Shower** - Cold temperatures immediately after your cool-down also help bring the heart rate down and increase circulation, which in turn helps reduce recovery time. The blood the heart pumped to meet the body's needs won't be allowed to pool in tired muscles, and those muscles will clear the lactic acid more quickly. It may also help to minimise soft tissue inflammation.

" **Remember, just because the final whistle has gone and you've won the match, this does not mean that your game is over** "

## COOL DOWN EXAMPLE

- 2 minutes light jogging.
- 3 minutes static stretching. Hold the stretches for 10-30 seconds, longer than the warm-up.
- Shake off each limb after stretching.

LOWER BACK

HEAD & NECK

SHOULDERS

CHEST

UPPER BACK

BICEPS

CALF

ONLY USE STATIC STRETCHING WHEN COOLING DOWN

TRICEPS

QUADRICEPS

HAMSTRING

OUTER THIGH

GLUTES

**STOMACH**

**BACK**

**SHOULDER**

**NECK**

**DELTOIDS**

**CHEST**

HAMSTRING

HIP FLEXOR

QUAD

GLUTES

CALF

GROIN

ONLY
static Stretch
When
cooling Down

# STRENGTH and CONDITIONING

## GUIDELINES FOR DEVELOPING STRENGTH AND CONDITIONING

Rugby players, particularly age grade players, come in every shape and size, and bring with them a wide range of natural athletic ability. Each player is an individual with specific strengths and specific weaknesses. For example, a young player may be quick over 40 metres but have little upper body strength. So when you begin to devise a strength and conditioning programme, each player should first be assessed individually to identify their strengths and weaknesses. Then you can build a programme appropriate to each player to help improve performance.

## "No Functional Screen... No Strength Training "

### FUNCTIONAL SCREENING

This assessment is sometimes called 'Functional Screening'. It identifies a player's deficiencies in movement, explains what's behind the deficiencies and offers ways to rectify them. The player is also given a score for how they move, which is an objective marker for comparison within the squad and for future assessment. You should seek advice from a qualified 'Strength & Conditioning Coach' about how to assess and measure deficiencies. The screening should uncover any issues about stability or movement, and a well-designed conditioning programme will strengthen the weak muscles and loosen the tight ones.

### SPORT-SPECIFIC TRAINING CIRCUIT

Certain types of fitness work can be particularly appropriate to a given sport. Equally, the fitness work should be appropriate to the player's age, current fitness and their ultimate goals.

Factors to be considered when designing a training circuit for rugby would be:
1. The skills required for the sport.
2. The fitness level required.
3. Actions or movements required, like jumping movements, or getting up quickly.
4. The major muscle groups used in the patterns of movement in the game.
5. The time of year, for example, preseason or competitive training.

### AN EXAMPLE OF A RUGBY-SPECIFIC CIRCUIT

| Circuits | Time on (secs) | Time off (secs) | Number |
|---|---|---|---|
| 1. Squat jump-to-catch | 30 | 15 | 3 |
| 2. Zigzag running | 30 | 15 | 3 |
| 3. Press-up | 30 | 15 | 3 |
| 4. Shuttle running | 30 | 15 | 3 |
| 5. Lunging with ball in front | 30 | 15 | 3 |

**STRENGTH PROGRESSION IN PRACTICAL SESSIONS FOR 10-12 YEAR OLDS**

These young players should begin simple resistance training with body weight exercises - i.e., the player's own weight provides the resistance for the movement; free weights are not needed. They should also begin learning the most basic proper technique for lifting weights.

1. Push-ups.
2. Pull-ups (hanging or horizontal).
3. Abdominal curls/Sit-ups.
4. Back raises.
5. Free squats.
6. Lunges.
7. Step-ups.

> " **Circuit training is designed to develop all-round physical and cardiovascular fitness** "

**STRENGTH PROGRESSION IN PRACTICAL SESSIONS FOR 13-15 YEAR OLDS**

Body weight exercises are still suitable for this age group, but they can also focus on standard dumbbell exercises using light loads. If they don't have dumbbells, one or two-litre bottles of water can be used.

1. Barbell squats or leg press.
2. Bench press with barbell or dumbbells.
3. Lunges with dumbbells.
4. Upright rowing with barbell.
5. Back extension or 'Good Mornings'.
6. Shoulder press with barbell or dumbbells.

You could also try the 'Fireman's Lift' with a team-mate of equal size, or jockey back races.

**STRENGTH PROGRESSION IN PRACTICAL SESSIONS FOR 16-18 YEAR OLDS**

It is essential players are properly trained in how to lift weights before they attempt to build strength or power, or start an intensive muscle-building regime.

1. Work on their technique with the core exercises, for example, squat, deadlift and clean.
2. Continue to build a basic foundation of strength.
3. Design exercises specific to each individual's needs, for example, to correct any imbalances.
4. Incorporate general strength training of the smaller, stabilising muscles used for a player's on-field position.

# SPEED anD AGILITY

In the same way we use repeated exercises to help young players build strength, we can also improve their speed and agility with similar repetition. Although a child develops their most fundamental level of speed-of-reaction — or reflexes - even before school age, these skills can also improve dramatically later in childhood, particularly around puberty, ages 11-13.

Agility is defined as the ability to change the direction and movement of the body as smoothly and efficiently as possible. This requires a combination of skills, including balance, speed, strength and co-ordination.

## GUIDELINES FOR SPEED AND AGILITY DRILLS

The key here is quality, not quantity. Keep the sprints short, and rest fully between sets. For best results:

1. Warm up thoroughly. These drills will not leave the players out of breath, but they do put a strain on the muscles.

2. Conduct the drills either on separate days from other training, or to begin a session after the warm-up.

3. A typical session would be 5 sets of 10 repetitions. The work-to-rest ratio is 1:5, so a five-second sprint should be followed by 25 seconds recovery.

4. Two sessions a week should be adequate in preseason, with one weekly session during the competitive season.

5. The drills which follow can be used for many sports. You can adapt them to make them more specific to rugby. Use two or three per session.

## "All types of speed can be trained through coaching and practice"

Speed is the ability to move quickly not only from position to position, but to accelerate, to change direction, and to simultaneously blend in a skilled movement, such as passing or kicking.

## FOR RUGBY, THE TYPES OF SPEED TO FOCUS ON ARE:

1. Quickness.
2. Acceleration/Deceleration.
3. Agility - change of direction and pace.
4. A high top-speed pace.
5. An ability to reproduce the speed repeatedly.
6. Endurance - to reproduce the speed in high-intensity with little recovery.

## PRACTICAL DRILLS FOR SPEED AND AGILITY

### BASIC SPRINTS

Set two cones 10-20 metres apart. Sprint from one to the next, and slowly jog back to the start. To make it more specific for rugby, for example, face backwards, lie down, then jump up to pretend to receive a pass.

### ROLLING START

Same as sprints, but jog for 10 metres before sprinting. This is designed to improve acceleration rather than speed off the mark. Also try running backwards or side-stepping.

### UPHILL SPRINTS

In competition, the first few strides are crucial. Running up a slight hill, about 30 degrees, helps to develop power and acceleration. Keep the distance short, 10-15 metres, and allow extra rest between sets.

### DOWNHILL SPRINTS

These help to develop leg speed and co-ordination and agility. This is sometimes known as over-speed training. Keep the distance short and ensure the hill has only a slight incline.

### HOLLOW SPRINTS

Set five cones out at 30 metre intervals. Sprint 30m, jog 30m, sprint 30m, jog 30m. Walk back to the start and repeat.

### CRUISE AND SPRINT

Mark out 100 metres. From the start, gradually accelerate to hit full speed at 60 metres, then sprint all-out the final 40 metres. Reduce the number of repetitions as it takes longer to complete.

### THE SNAKE

Set up 6-8 cones in a line about one metre apart. Weave through the cones, turn, and weave back.

### FOLLOW THE LEADER

You need a training partner and a large area. Have the partner jog, run and sprint randomly over a large area, while you shadow them as closely as possible. This is an excellent drill to work on reaction time, acceleration and speed endurance.

### LADDER DRILLS

A ladder is a simple device to improve leg-speed and co-ordination. It can be used for a number of speed and agility drills.

# CORE CONDITIONING

## GUIDELINES FOR DEVELOPING CORE CONDITIONING

Always concentrate on good form and technique when exercising. For these exercises, ensure you have the correct alignment and posture - whether standing, lying or seated - before you start work.

## NEUTRAL ALIGNMENT (TA)

Practice standing in a neutral stance, for example, a good posture. This allows the body to support itself with the minimum stress. Poor posture is usually related to poor alignment. Check the head and neck, shoulders, abdomen and lower back are aligned.

## BREATHING

Try to breathe in a relaxed manner throughout the exercise. The temptation is to hold one's breath, but by focusing on your breathing you will develop a more relaxed approach to training.

## "SCOOPING"

This is an important - and difficult - abdominal movement to master. It means drawing the lower abdomen back in towards the spine. The intention is to stabilise the trunk by engaging the Transverse Abdominis (TA) muscle complex. One position to use is to lie on your back, knees bent to 90 degrees with thighs perpendicular to the floor. This allows you to flatten the back against the floor while 'Scooping the TA'.

> **Walk tall, shoulders back, chest out, head up**

You need to practice this daily. It is a subtle movement, and a coach will need to spend time with the players to make sure they are doing it correctly.

## COMMON ERRORS WHEN CARRYING OUT CORE EXERCISES

1. Chin poking out or head too forward.
2. Hips flexing.
3. Back arching.
4. Excessive abdominal push.

> **You too can be a 'SUPERMAN'**

## LEVEL I

A basic core training routine that challenges the player is to complete three of these simple stability exercises. This should be done daily for a week or two, aiming to develop a habit of daily stability training. The player should hold these positions for up to 60 seconds and repeat 3 times.

### PRESS-UP

Hold a straight body position, supported on flat hands and toes. Brace the abdominals, and maintain a straight line from head to toe. Lower the body to 5 inches, maintaining a straight line, then return to starting position.

### PLANK

Hold a straight body position, supported by elbows and toes. Brace the abdominals and hold the straight line.

### SIDE PLANK

Lie on the side, with the top hip directly above the lower hip. Push up until there is a straight body position. Keep the elbow under the shoulder. Lower slowly, and repeat on other side.

### BRIDGE

Lie on the floor with knees bent and feet flat. Squeeze the gluteals, then push the hips up until there is a straight line through knee and hip to upper body, while shoulders remain on the floor.

### SUPERMAN

Kneel, and place hands below shoulders and knees below hips. Extend right leg back and left arm forward, while maintaining a straight body line throughout. Repeat with opposite limbs.

## LEVEL II

### CORE CONDITIONING WITH SWISS-BALL

This work challenges both hip and shoulder cores. Again, exercises are mainly static. The programme should be a progression and performed daily. Hold positions for 15 seconds and increase to 30 seconds.

**SWISS-BALL**

## LEVEL III

### CORE CONDITIONING WITH WOBBLE OR BALANCE BOARD

This level progresses from static to dynamic stability. It also moves on to upright stability exercises which are becoming more sport specific than static patterns. Ensure core control at all times. Perform for as long as possible, and follow the manufacturer's instructions. Move on to using one leg, or increase the time spent balancing.

**WOBBLE BOARD**

**LEVEL IV**

**CORE CONDITIONING WITH WEIGHTS**

Carry out the very basic ground exercises, this time with weights. Focus always on good balance.

**DUMBBELLS**

1. Use a dumbbell, kettlebell or med-ball.
2. Hold position for a count of between 5 and 10 seconds.
3. Increase the weight only when you feel comfortable.

**KETTLEBELL**

**MED-BALL**

# SAFETY and EQUIPMENT

One of your primary responsibilities as a coach is to ensure, as best you can, that your players are safe. Before a training session or a match, try to anticipate any potential hazard, for example, the venue may have nearby walls or footpaths, or the condition of the playing surface may be questionable.

In any session, be sure the work done is appropriate to the age and skill level of your players, and that drills are performed along recommended lines.

Equally, players must be made aware that they have their own responsibilities in terms of safety.

One simple way to manage the health and safety of your charges is to remember the acronym 'PEACE of mind'.

## P is for PLAYERS

**Clothing and Equipment**. Before training or a match, have a quick check of the players' gear. Ensure any jewellery, such as wristwatches or earrings, is removed. Be sure the appropriate boots and studs are worn, even for training. **NEVER** let someone play or train without a gum shield.

> Tell your Coach if you have any Medical Condition or Allergies

**Fitness.** Clearly, you should not force anyone to play. Equally, be aware some players will try to hide an injury in order to get out there. Be careful that a 'fun' session doesn't get slightly out of control and overly physical or aggressive.

**Medical history.** Rugby is a physical game, and there are going to be injuries. To ensure your players get the most appropriate treatment as quickly as possible, **always** carry up-to-date medical records for your players. This should include information such as allergies or underlying conditions, and even more crucial information such as blood type or current medication.

## E is for EQUIPMENT

Compared to many sports, rugby has a whole range of equipment used in training, from tackle bags to scrum machines, sledges, elastic ropes or hurdles. A regular, routine check will ensure they pose no potential danger. Always check the post protectors: be sure the edges have not become too worn and abrasive. Follow the manufacturer's instructions for maintaining the scrum machines.

## "Always wear a Gum Shield"

### A is for AREA

As mentioned above, always walk through the training or playing area before getting started to check for potential dangers, such as uneven ground, debris, or nearby walls or footpaths.

The weather, obviously, can also play a part. A simple test to check whether the ground is too hard - whether from cold or heat - is to punch it with your fist: if it hurts, imagine a player's head smacking down on it.

### C is for CRUCIAL INFORMATION

All matters to do with health and safety should be clearly signposted around the ground or in the clubhouse. This will help everyone: players, visitors, officials or staff.

**Always Dress for the weather Be it very cold, wet or warm**

### E is for EMERGENCY POINTS

Always ensure any training or playing venue has easy access for emergency vehicles. Emergency telephone numbers should be clearly displayed. Indeed, your school or club's insurance policy may stipulate that you carry a working mobile phone during training, matches, or while travelling.

### Equipment Safety Checklist

1. Tackle bags and ruck
2. Post protectors
3. Corner flags
4. Personal equipment (e.g. Mouth guards, headgear)
5. First Aid Kit

# STAGING a MATCH

If your club or school is playing host to a competitive match or similar event, make sure the venue is properly prepared. Make sure everyone involved is fully aware of the arrangements which have been made.

## MEDICAL

You **must** have someone with first aid experience in attendance, preferably a doctor. If possible, have an ambulance at the ground, and ensure it has easy access in and out. Inform the nearest hospital emergency room in advance that the match is to be played, and have the telephone number to hand. Every club/school medical room should have a spinal board, hard neck collar and large first aid kit. Have ice bags ready on the sideline.

Fail to Prepare, Prepare to Fail

## FACILITIES

1. Ensure the clubhouse is open for supporters and officials.
2. Ensure the changing rooms, showers and toilets are clean.
3. The playing area should be cleared and safe and marked out for the match, i.e, touchline flags and goalpost protectors in place.
4. Ensure no spectators get in to the playing area during the match.
5. Ensure there are adequate and appropriate refreshments available for after the match.

## "In short, treat your visitors as you would like to be treated"

## REFEREE

If it is your responsibility to ensure a referee is available to officiate, you should contact them no later than 24 hours before kick-off.

## WHAT SHOULD A SPORTS FIRST AID KIT CONTAIN?

No youth sports team or club should be without a First Aid kit which is equipped to treat the most common injuries and illnesses.  The type of first aid that may be required varies by sport. Because bruises, abrasions and sprained ankles are more common in rugby, a team's first aid kit, for instance, needs to be stocked with cold packs, elastic bandages and plasters. (In contrast, a track team's kit would need supplies to treat blisters, abrasions, pulled muscles and sprains).

If your team is going to be training or playing in the sun, carry sunscreen, and perhaps an allergy kit to manage insect bites.

Stock a realistic supply: Be prepared to treat more than one child at an event.

**Easy Access:** First Aid supplies should be kept close at hand, and clearly marked to allow rapid identification. Use clear plastic bags within the kit to store extra materials and to sort your supplies. For instance, it is helpful to partition supplies into modules, such as open wound care, muscular care, and so forth.

**First Aid Bag:** Carry First Aid supplies in a watertight bag or box which can withstand rough handling and extreme temperatures. Ensure the bag is zipped and equipped for the worst of weather.

**First Aid Kit:** Listed below are the items recommended for a sports First Aid kit. Go through the list carefully and decide which items are most appropriate for your specific needs. Have a medical professional teach you how to take care of your players, so that when the time comes you will know, for example, how to apply a Steri-Strip to close a wound, form a sling to support an arm or shoulder injury, or use a pocket mask to perform rescue breathing.

**General Supplies**
1.  First Aid Manual or Emergency/CPR flashcards.
2.  Safety pins.
3.  Bandage scissors.
4.  Tweezers.
5.  Standard oral thermometer: digital, mercury, or alcohol.
6.  Wooden tongue depressors.
7.  Waterproof flashlight (and spare batteries).
8.  CPR mouth barrier or pocket mask.
9.  Sterile (hypoallergenic or latex or non-latex ) surgical gloves (at least 2 pair).
10.  Instant chemical cold pack(s).
11.  Sealable bags (Ziploc), to hold ice.
12.  Rescue blanket or foil wrap.
13.  Mobile phone.
14.  List of emergency phone numbers (local GP, nearest hospital and fire station).

## Wound Care Preparations and Dressings

1. Elastic bandages in assorted sizes (strip, knuckle and broad); cloth with adhesive is preferable.
2. Adhesive strips for wound closure (Steri-Strip), assorted sizes, reinforced or elastic.
3. 3x3" or 4x4" highly absorbent sterile gauze pads.
4. 5x9" or 8x10" sterile gauze ('trauma') pads.
5. Nonstick sterile bandages in assorted sizes (used to cover abrasions).
6. 1", 2", 3" and 4" rolled conforming gauze.
7. 1"x 10yds (9.1m) rolled cloth adhesive tape.
8. 1"x 10yds (9.1m) rolled waterproof adhesive tape.
9. Safe Skin (4⅛in x 3⅜in).
10. Moleskin Plus (4⅛in x 3⅜in).
11. Cotton Wool.
12. Sterile cotton-tipped swabs or applicators, 2 per package.
13. Povidone-iodine 10% solution.

## Splinting and Sling Material

1. Cravat cloth (triangular bandage).
2. 2", 3", and 4" elastic wrap.
3. Aluminium finger splints.

## Eye Medications and Dressings

1. Eye bandages.
2. Individual sterile oval eye pads.

## Skin Preparations

1. Insect repellent.
2. Sunscreen lotion or cream (SPF 15 or 30).

## Non-prescription Medications

1. Decongestant nasal spray (to treat a nosebleed that doesn't respond to pressure).
2. Liquid glucose or chocolate bar, to treat a hypoglycemic - low blood sugar reaction.

## Other

Other equipment and supplies may be available at the venue, but are not usually transported with a youth team, unless there are special circumstances. These include such items as large splints to accommodate major fractures, stretcher, and an AED (Automated External Defibrillator).

Rugby is a physical sport – and for most players that is part of the appeal of the game.

But, inevitably, there will be injuries. Fortunately, the vast majority of injuries at age level are minor and easy to treat. You can help to keep injuries to a minimum by making sure of the following:

1. The basic skills of the game are taught properly.
2. The pitch is safe, particularly in winter.
3. The players are matched to their age group.
4. The players are fully warmed up before contact.

## SPRAINS AND STRAINS

At any level of the game, the most common injuries are soft tissue bruising and sprains, usually caused by a direct blow. Most players recover fairly quickly and can play on. However, if the player feels unable to continue, they should be removed to the sideline and apply ice to the injured area for no more than five minutes.

**"A coach should never encourage - or badger a player to continue against their will"**

## WRIST, SHOULDER, KNEE AND ANKLE INJURIES

Most injuries to the rest of the body are to the main joints.

Because the bones of children are softer and more flexible than those of adults, they are particularly susceptible to what are called 'green stick fractures'. These often occur in the wrist. A green stick fracture occurs when a bone bends and cracks, instead of breaking completely. They can be difficult to spot, as there may not be much pain or swelling

Never, ever, play with an injury

and the young player can use the limb and has full motion. Mild green stick fractures sometimes are thought to be sprains. Even mild green stick fractures usually require a cast. In addition to holding the cracked pieces of the bone together so they can heal, a cast can help prevent the bone from breaking all the way through in another fall.

If a young player complains of a shoulder injury, always suspect it could be a broken collarbone (clavicle), however slight. This often occurs when a player falls on an outstretched arm. Any movement of the shoulder is painful. The player should be taken for an x-ray immediately. Generally, a broken collarbone will heal in about six weeks.

### KNEE

It is unusual for a young player to get a significant knee injury, but any swelling of the joint should be treated seriously. The most common knee complaint among adolescents is when the knee cap (patella) tendon attached to the lower leg (tibia) becomes inflamed due to repeated stress. There will be pain just below the knee and some swelling. Initial treatment involves applying ice to the area, and then a full rest from training.

If you have a 'dead leg' or haematoma (bruising in muscle) DO NOT exercise or stretch the affected limb. Ensure that you apply **'PRICE'**: intermittently over 48 hours. i.e. **Pressure, Rest, Ice, Compression and Elevation.**

### ANKLE

Ankle ligaments can be easily damaged when the foot is forced to turn inside. The pain can be severe, and the ankle will swell according to the severity. If the player cannot put any weight on the foot, there may be a fracture. Again, an x-ray may be required.
If a young player has trouble sleeping after injuring a limb, the possibility of a fracture should be investigated.

### CUTS

The biggest concern with this type of injury (laceration) is infection. Any open wound over a joint, or which exposes the bone, or which requires stitches, should be dealt with as soon as possible, probably with a visit to the local Accident and Emergency (A&E) department.

### TEETH

No player should be allowed onto the pitch without a well-fitted mouth guard. Sometimes a tooth which is knocked out can be re-implanted. Keep the tooth moist, and get the player to a dentist.

### HEAD INJURIES

In recent years there has been a heavy emphasis, at every level of the sport, on the increased incidence of concussion. Players are bigger than ever and the hits are harder than ever. This applies even at age grade rugby. Study the concussion section for more detailed information.

At this level of the game, any player who seems even slightly affected by a bang to the head - appears dazed or unsteady on their feet - should be taken off the pitch temporarily and assessed.

Ask them to answer simple questions - What day is it? What team are we playing? Check their concentration by asking them to repeat backwards a series of numbers: 419 (914 is correct).

If they struggle with the tasks, or are even slow to respond, remove them from the game/ training completely. Do not leave the player unattended.

In a serious incident, a player may lose consciousness. In this case, merely as a precaution you must operate as if the player has a neck or spine injury. Immediately remove the gum shield and ensure the player is breathing properly. Call for the ambulance. While waiting, do not move the player, and keep them warm.

## HEART ATTACK

Mercifully, this is a rare event, but it does occur. Call the emergency services immediately. Every club or school should have a defibrillator easily accessible, and at all times at least one member of the available coaching staff should be trained in how to use it. **If you plan to be involved in coaching, you should learn CPR.**

## CARDIOPULMONARY RESUSCITATION (CPR)

### 1.  Call
Check for unresponsiveness. If the person is not responsive and not breathing or not breathing normally,  call 999 and return to the victim. In most locations the emergency dispatcher can assist you with CPR instructions.

### 2.  Pump
If the victim is still not breathing normally, coughing or moving, begin chest compressions. Push down in the centre of the chest 2 inches 30 times. Pump down in the centre of the chest 2 inches 30 times.  Pump hard and fast at the rate of at least 100/minute, faster than once per second.

### 3.  Blow
Tilt the head back and lift the chin. Pinch nose and cover the mouth with yours and blow until you see the chest rise.  Give 2 breaths.  Each breath should take 1 second.

## CONTINUE WITH 30 PUMPS AND 2 BREATHS UNTIL HELP ARRIVES

**NOTE:** This ratio is the same for one-person & two-person CPR.  The person pumping the chest stops while the other gives mouth-to-mouth breathing.

Throughout this guide we have emphasised that the focus should be on fun. But, in fact, your prime responsibility as a coach is to your players' **SAFETY**.

## WHAT IS CONCUSSION?

Concussion is, technically, a "traumatic brain injury". The brain is a delicate instrument, a spongy mass of nerve cells encased in three thin membranes and cushioned in a fluid. All of this is protected by the skull, or cranium. When the body is hit with enough force that the brain is shifted to collide with the cranium, concussion can occur.

Concussion can have a significant effect on both the short- and long-term health of a player if not managed correctly.

> **There is no such thing as a minor concussion or 'knock to the head'**

## WHAT CAUSES CONCUSSION?

Concussion can be caused by a blow to the head, or body, and from whiplash movements of the head and neck, when a player is tackled or collides with another player or with the ground. Remember, **a player doesn't need to be hit in the head to sustain a concussion**; a hit to the body can transmit force to the head.

It is also important to remember that, immediately following a suspected concussion, the brain is particularly susceptible to further significant damage from another impact. This is called **second impact syndrome**, when a player returns too quickly after an initial concussion. Even a minor second blow can set the effects in motion.

Because the brain is more vulnerable after an initial injury, it takes only a minimal force to cause irreversible damage. The brain's ability to self-regulate blood flow is impaired. The pressure to the brain increases rapidly, and can lead quickly to brain death.

Therefore the player **MUST** be immediately removed from the pitch, whether playing or training, and **MUST NOT** return until they have completed the graduated return to play (GRTP) protocol - see below.

## CONCUSSION FACTS

Most concussions do not involve loss of consciousness.
Concussions will not show up on CAT scans, MRI's or X-rays.
A concussion is invisible but the symptoms are not.
Some symptoms are visible days or weeks after the injury.
Multiple concussions can cause cumulative and long-lasting damage.

## CONCUSSION CLUES

There are some obvious visual clues as to whether a player has suffered some form of concussion. Is the player:
1. Lying motionless on ground.
2. Slow to get up.
3. Unsteady on feet.
4. Clutching head.
5. Looking dazed, blank or vacant.
6. Confused/Not aware of plays or events.
7. Possibly lost consciousness, even briefly.

## CONCUSSION SYMPTOMS

1. Confusion.
2. Dizziness or balance problems.
3. Headache.
4. Sensitive to light or noise.
5. Double or fuzzy vision.
6. Nausea or vomiting.
7. Feeling sluggish, hazy, groggy.
8. 'Don't feel right'.
9. Difficulty paying attention & remembering.

**NO TV, NO Texting, NO Computers, NO Reading**

Once the player has been removed from action, the first stage of the GRTP often involves asking the player a series of simple questions, for example:
1. What month is it?
2. What is the day of the week?
3. What time is it right now? (within 1 hour)
4. What venue are we at today?
5. Which half is it now?
6. Who scored last in this match?
7. What team did we play last week/game?

The signs and symptoms of concussion usually start at the time of the injury, but the onset of these may be delayed for up to 24–48 hours. Coaches, team-mates, parents and friends should be aware of the signs and symptoms of a concussed player.

## GRADUATED RETURN TO PLAY (GRTP) PROTOCOL

Players can move on to the next stage only after they have been symptom-free during the full period of each stage. If they are not symptom-free, they must stay at that stage until they are. (Note: in serious cases this could take a week)

| Rehabilitation Stage | Functional Exercise at Stage | Objective |
|---|---|---|
| Stage 1:<br>No activity | Symptom-limited physical and cognitive rest | Recovery |
| Stage 2:<br>Light aerobic exercise | Walking, limited exercise intensity | Increase heart rate |
| Stage 3:<br>Sport-specific exercise | Running/Passing drills | Add movement |
| Stage 4:<br>Non-contact<br>training drills | Progress to complex drills<br>May start progressive resistance training | Add coordination<br>and thought |
| Stage 5:<br>Full-contact practice | Following medical clearance<br>Participate in normal training activities | Restore confidence |
| Stage 6:<br>Return to play | Full Participation | Confident |

## NO Bright Lights &
## NO Physical Exertion

## WHAT IS ESSENTIAL?

What is essential for a session, and what would be "nice to have"?

Consider just exactly what you really need for training. Do you need ruck pads, tackle tubes and tackle suits (or ladders, poles, scrum machines)? If you're not careful, you could bring a whole lorry's worth of unnecessary equipment to training.

But this is an essential list.

Your starting point is: what do you need for a session or match?

Be sure you know where the equipment is kept, how to get your hands on it and whether you need to 'book' it if other teams are sharing the equipment.

- 2-10 x Balls
- 10-20 x Cones
- 10-15 x Bibs
- 2-6 x Bottles of Water
- Set of Studs and Spanner bag
- A Mobile Phone

- A Pump and Adaptor
- The Medical Kit
- Your Training Plan
- Your Emergency Plan
- A Whistle & Stopwatch

| Player's Name | Training Sessions Attended | | | | | | | | | | | | | |
|---|---|---|---|---|---|---|---|---|---|---|---|---|---|---|
| | 1 | 2 | 3 | 4 | 5 | 6 | 7 | 8 | 9 | 10 | 11 | 12 | 13 | 14 |
| | | | | | | | | | | | | | | |
| | | | | | | | | | | | | | | |
| | | | | | | | | | | | | | | |
| | | | | | | | | | | | | | | |
| | | | | | | | | | | | | | | |
| | | | | | | | | | | | | | | |
| | | | | | | | | | | | | | | |
| | | | | | | | | | | | | | | |
| | | | | | | | | | | | | | | |
| | | | | | | | | | | | | | | |
| | | | | | | | | | | | | | | |
| | | | | | | | | | | | | | | |
| | | | | | | | | | | | | | | |
| | | | | | | | | | | | | | | |
| | | | | | | | | | | | | | | |
| | | | | | | | | | | | | | | |
| | | | | | | | | | | | | | | |
| | | | | | | | | | | | | | | |
| | | | | | | | | | | | | | | |
| | | | | | | | | | | | | | | |
| | | | | | | | | | | | | | | |
| | | | | | | | | | | | | | | |
| | | | | | | | | | | | | | | |
| | | | | | | | | | | | | | | |

There are 4 codes to be used: **A** = Justified Absence    **X** = Unjustified Absence    **I** = Injured    **P** = Present

| Player's Name | Player's Mobile No. | Email | Guardian's Name | Contact No. |
|---|---|---|---|---|
| | | | | |
| | | | | |
| | | | | |
| | | | | |
| | | | | |
| | | | | |
| | | | | |
| | | | | |
| | | | | |
| | | | | |
| | | | | |
| | | | | |
| | | | | |

# SAMPLE SESSION PLANNER

| TEAM: | NUMBERS: | CONDITIONS: |
|---|---|---|
| DATE: | TIME: | DURATION: |

| | |
|---|---|
| WARM UP | Session Objectives |
| | For INDIVIDUALS |
| Equipment Required | |
| | For UNITS |
| COOL DOWN | |
| | For the TEAM |

**Session Outline**

| KEY DRILLS / GAMES | POST SESSION COMMENTS |
|---|---|
| INJURIES | ABSENTEES |
| SUMMARISE | ANY OTHER BUSINESS |

| TEAM: | DATE: | KICK OFF: |
|---|---|---|
| OPPONENTS: | VENUE: | MATCH TYPE: |

| THE GAME PLAN<br>Our STRENGTHS | Their STRENGTHS |
|---|---|
| Weather Tactics (Sun/Wind/Rain) | Their WEAKNESS |

**Key Talking Points**

1.

2.

3.

**Referee Notes**

1.

2.

3.

## SAMPLE TIMETABLE

| Time | Theme | The Warm Up |
|---|---|---|
| 3.00pm | Kick-off | *Approximately 35 minutes of Preparation Time can be used on the following:* |
| 2.58pm | Run-on | |
| 2.55pm | Captains say 'Last Words' | → Individual Stretching Time |
| 2.52pm | Coach Addresses Team | → Team Warm-up Time |
| 2.50pm | Team Returns to Dressing Room | → Player/Coach Time |
| 2.15pm | Team heads out for Warm-up | → Specialist Unit Time |
| 2.00pm | Team Changes into Kit | (Kickers, Hookers, Scrumhalf) |
| 1.45pm | Players get Strapping on | → Unit Time (Backs & Forwards) |
| 1.30pm | Team Briefing | → Team Contact Time |
| 1.20pm | Venue Familiarisation | → Team Time |
| 1.15pm | Arrive and Meet at Venue | |

# SAMPLE MATCH RECORD

| TEAM SHEET | Try (T) Conv. (C) Pen. (P) | SCORERS | NOTES |
|---|---|---|---|

OPPONENTS _____

VENUE

REFEREE _____

DATE _____ K.O. TIME

| TEAM SHEET | Try (T) Conv. (C) Pen. (P) | SCORERS | NOTES |
|---|---|---|---|
| 15 | | | **Pre-match** |
| 14 | | | |
| 13 | | | |
| 12 | | | |
| 11 | | | |
| 10 | | | |
| 9 | | | Half-time |
| 8 | | | |
| 7 | | | |
| 6 | | | |
| 5 | | | |
| 4 | | | |
| 3 | | | Full-time |
| 2 | | | |
| 1 | | | |
| REPLACEMENTS | | ON FOR | |
| 16 | | | |
| 17 | | | |
| 18 | | | RESULT AT: |
| 19 | | | Half-time: |
| 20 | | | Full-time: |
| 21 | | | After Extra-time: |
| 22 | | | |
| 23 | | | MAN OF THE MATCH |

Available to download from www.passporttosport.com

100

# MATCH OBSERVATION SHEET

| TEAM: | | DATE: | |
|---|---|---|---|
| OPPONENTS: | | VENUE: | |

| | Strengths | Weaknesses |
|---|---|---|
| **YOUR ATTACK**<br>Gaining possession<br>Going forward<br>Support<br>Rucks and Mauls<br>Turnovers (Lost ball by your Team)<br>Pressure and possession<br>Field position and pace | | |
| **YOUR DEFENCE**<br>Contesting possession<br>Applying pressure by tackling<br>Preventing territorial gain<br>Support<br>Turnovers (Ball won by your Team)<br>Counter-attack | | |

## SET-PIECE

| | | | |
|---|---|---|---|
| Scrums - Attacking : Clean ball? | Won | 1 2 3 4 5 | Lost 1 2 3 4 5 |
|       - Defending : Challenging? | Won | 1 2 3 4 5 | Lost 1 2 3 4 5 |
| Lineouts - Attacking : Clean ball? | Won | 1 2 3 4 5 | Lost 1 2 3 4 5 |
|       - Defending : Challenging? | Won | 1 2 3 4 5 | Lost 1 2 3 4 5 |

| | | | | |
|---|---|---|---|---|
| Tackling: | Good | 1 2 3 4 5 6 7 8 9 10 | Bad | 1 2 3 4 5 6 7 8 9 10 |
| Rucks: | Won | 1 2 3 4 5 6 7 8 9 10 | Lost | 1 2 3 4 5 6 7 8 9 10 |
| Penalties: | Won | 1 2 3 4 5 6 7 8 9 10 | Conceeded | 1 2 3 4 5 6 7 8 9 10 |
| Communication: Good / Bad / Average | | | Passing: Good / Bad / Average | |

## SUMMARISE

# SELF-ASSESSMENT FORM

| BEHAVIOUR | DETAIL | COMMENT |
|---|---|---|
| **MANAGEMENT/ ORGANISATION** | Set-up activities | |
| | Smooth transitions | |
| | Max. use of resources | |
| | Variety | |
| | Positioning | |
| **COMMUNICATION** | Clarity/simplicity | |
| | Good use of voice | |
| | Active listening | |
| | Positive feedback | |
| | Negative feedback | |
| **TEACHING** | Explanations | |
| | Demonstrations | |
| | Progressions | |
| | Error identifications | |
| | Error corrections | |
| **APPLICATION OF KNOWLEDGE** | Task specific exercise | |
| | Relevant exercises | |
| | Exercise identification & use | |
| | Principles of play | |
| **OBSERVATIONS** | | |
| | | |
| | | |
| | | |

| COACH | DATE | AGE / LEVEL |
|---|---|---|
| OBSERVER · | SIGNED | |

PASSPORT TO RUGBY

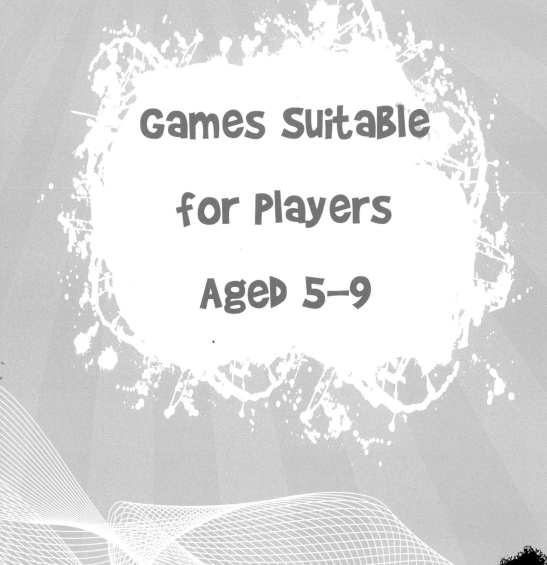

Games Suitable

for Players

Aged 5–9

# RUGBY GAMES

**ALL** | **25x25**

| DIRECTION OF RUN | GROUND COVERED | PASS | TRY LINE |
|---|---|---|---|

## IDEAL FOR IMPROVING AGILITY

## GAME NOTES

➜ Create a large playing area.

➜ Stay inside the marked out area.

➜ Get your players to pair up.

➜ In each pair, one leads and the other follows.

➜ The leader must try to lose the follower.

➜ Shout 'STOP' after 15 seconds to see if the leader managed to lose his follower.

➜ Continue the exercise by swapping the pairs.

## THE SET UP

➜ Depending on numbers, start with 25m x 25m.

➜ 4 cones and a ball.

➜ Whole squad.

## HOW TO SCORE?

➜ When you call stop, count the paces between each leader and follower.

## WHAT TO CALL OUT

➜ "Look for space to run into"

➜ "Take small steps when changing direction"

➜ "Keep looking where you are going"

➜ "Look to see what is going on around you"

➜ "Move your body to lose your follower"

## Coaching Notes

✔ Vary the Times before calling 'STOP'.

✔ Vary the drill to include hopping.

✔ Vary the Rest period between races.

**1**

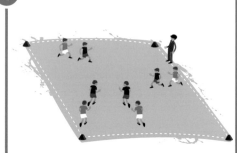

Start the game by pairing off the teams, ensure you have even numbers.

**2**

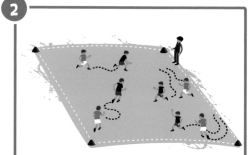

When you shout 'GO' each player must follow his partner or leader and stay within 1 metre.

**3**

Vary the game from running, to hopping on either leg or bounding with both legs together.

**WHOLE SQUAD GAME**
## cat and mouse

| DIRECTION OF RUN | GROUND COVERED | PASS | TRY LINE |
| --- | --- | --- | --- |

## IDEAL FOR IMPROVING AGILITY

### GAME NOTES

➜ Make 20% of the squad 'Cats'.

➜ Give each 'Cat' a ball.

➜ The 'Cats' turn 'Mice' into 'Cats' by touching them with the ball.

➜ 'Cats' must hold the ball in both hands.

➜ No Throwing of the ball is allowed.

➜ To become a 'Mouse' again, players touched must stand with legs apart and transitioned by another player crawling under.

### THE SET UP

➜ 25m x 35m - depending on numbers.

➜ A ball for each 'Cat', also a bib if available.

➜ Whole squad.

### HOW TO SCORE?

➜ 2 points for each player turned into a 'Mouse'.

➜ 6 bonus points if all turned into 'Mice'.

### WHAT TO CALL OUT

➜ "Keep moving into space"

➜ "Don't move in straight lines"

➜ "Keep looking around at what is happening"

➜ "Remember short fast feet"

### coaching notes

✔ Teaching your players how to move with speed in a confined area will get them out of tight situations when surrounded by defenders.

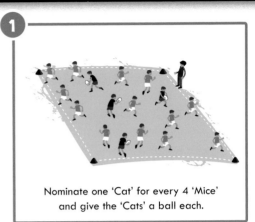

Nominate one 'Cat' for every 4 'Mice' and give the 'Cats' a ball each.

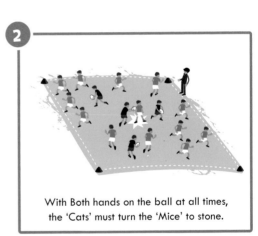

With Both hands on the ball at all times, the 'Cats' must turn the 'Mice' to stone.

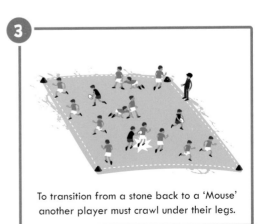

To transition from a stone back to a 'Mouse' another player must crawl under their legs.

SMALL SIDED GAME
## Jolly Roger

4V4    10X6

| DIRECTION OF RUN | GROUND COVERED | PASS | TRY LINE |
|---|---|---|---|

## IDEAL FOR IMPROVING AGILITY

### GAME NOTES
➡ Make 2 teams at opposite sides of the playing area.
➡ 1 team is called the 'Pirates'.
➡ The other team is called the 'Navy'.
➡ The ball is the 'Treasure'.
➡ The First Pirate (called 'The Jolly Roger') must escape with the 'Treasure' (ball) either to the end or past the first set of cones to the side.
➡ If they is two-handed touched they rejoins the 'Pirates'.

### THE SET UP
➡ 10m long x 6m wide.
➡ 6 cones, a ball, bibs and tag-belts if available.
➡ 8 - two teams of 4.

### HOW TO SCORE?
➡ 2 points if the Pirate escapes to the side.
➡ 5 points if he reaches the opposite end.
➡ 1 point to the Navy for every Pirate caught.

### WHAT TO CALL OUT
➡ "Look for space to run into"
➡ "Take small steps when changing direction"
➡ "Explode into the space, if it is there"
➡ "Look to see what is going on around you"

### COACHING NOTES
✔ Swap the 'Pirates' and the 'Navy' around after each 'Pirate' has been a 'Jolly Roger'.

**1**
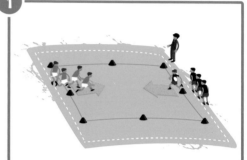
Divide the team up into 2 groups - 1 called the 'Navy' the other called the 'Pirates'.

**2**
The head 'Pirate' called the 'Jolly Roger' must get to the other end with the ball 'Treasure'.

**3**
If he is two-handed tackled, or he loses the 'Treasure' to the 'Navy', he rejoins the 'Pirates'.

# RUGBY GAMES

WHOLE SQUAD GAME
## Criss Cross

## IDEAL FOR IMPROVING PASSING AND HANDLING

### GAME NOTES

→ Create even numbers of players at 8 cones set out at each corner and in the middle of the playing area.
→ The lead player in each group should have a ball.
→ On your whistle, each ball-carrier runs across the square to the group opposite them.
→ Each ball-carrier passes the ball to the first player in the group opposite them.
→ They repeat this, running to the opposite group without banging into one another.

### THE SET UP

→ 15m x 15m square.
→ 8 cones, a ball, bibs or similar coloured jerseys.
→ Depending on numbers - 4 to 6 per station.

### HOW TO SCORE?

→ 1 point for each group who completes a set without dropping the ball or banging into other groups.

### WHAT TO CALL OUT

→ "Keep the ball in two hands"
→ "Look where you are going"
→ "See what is going on around you"
→ "Look to see what is going on around you"

### Coaching Notes

✔ If numbers are limited, reduce the number of stations to 4.

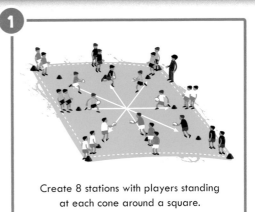

Create 8 stations with players standing at each cone around a square.

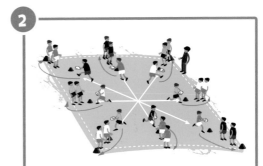

Give each player at the front a ball to run diagonally without banging into each other.

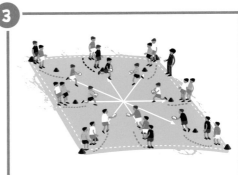

Players must pass the ball to the opposite player without dropping the ball or crashing.

# RUGBY GAMES

**WHOLE SQUAD GAME**
## Asterix

**ALL** | **15×15**

---

| DIRECTION OF RUN | GROUND COVERED | PASS | TRY LINE |
|---|---|---|---|

## IDEAL FOR IMPROVING PASSING AND HANDLING

### GAME NOTES

➜ This drill is set up similarly to 'Criss Cross'.

➜ The exception is that after each player completes a set, they change the exercise.

➜ For example: pop pass, rolls the ball, long pass, place the ball, pass off left and right.

➜ Instead of running straight, they might follow their pass or choose the group to pass to.

### THE SET UP

➜ 15m x 15m square.

➜ 8 cones, 8 balls, ball, bibs or similar coloured jerseys.

➜ Depending on numbers - 4 to 6 per station.

### HOW TO SCORE?

➜ 1 point for each group who completes a set without dropping the ball or banging into other groups.

### WHAT TO CALL OUT

➜ "Keep the ball in two hands"

➜ "Look where you are going"

➜ "See what is going on around you"

➜ "Concentrate on swinging the ball across the body to pass, rugby style"

➜ "Hands out and fingers spread"

### Coaching Notes

✔ Get your players to pop pass, roll it, place it at the feet or toss into the air.

✔ You can also get them to pass right and follow their pass.

✔ Get them thinking by passing to the right or left and running straight.

**1**

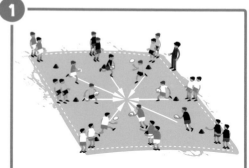

Similar to 'Criss Cross' except the style of pass changes after each player completes a turn.

**2**

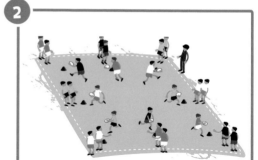

Vary the game to include, a pop pass, roll the ball, toss the ball and place the ball.

**3**

Further variation is possible with passing to the left or right and/or following their pass.

12+    8X8

DIRECTION OF RUN — GROUND COVERED — PASS — TRY LINE

## IDEAL FOR IMPROVING PASSING AND HANDLING

### GAME NOTES

➜ Divide the squad into 4 equal groups.

➜ Set them out with a ball at each corner of a square.

➜ The lead player must pass the ball clockwise around the square and follow his pass to the back of that group.

➜ You can introduce a second ball to make this drill more challenging, if it is too easy.

### THE SET UP

➜ 8m x 8m square.

➜ 4 cones and 4 balls.

➜ 4 to 6 per station.

➜ Set up two games if sufficient numbers.

### HOW TO SCORE?

➜ Use a stopwatch to see how long it takes to get a complete set done and back to their original station.

### WHAT TO CALL OUT

➜ "Keep the ball in two hands"

➜ "Swing the ball across the body"

➜ "Get your hands set to catch the pass"

➜ "Hit the target area with the pass"

### Coaching Notes

✔ Change the direction of the pass to anti-clockwise.

✔ To increase the intensity of the drill you can get the player passing the ball to run to the group after the group he passes it to.

✔ If able for this, get them to miss two groups and to complete a full round back to his original group if able to.

**1**

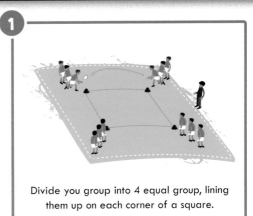

Divide you group into 4 equal group, lining them up on each corner of a square.

**2**

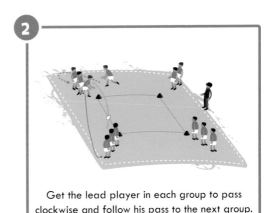

Get the lead player in each group to pass clockwise and follow his pass to the next group.

**3**

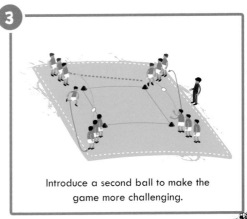

Introduce a second ball to make the game more challenging.

# RUGBY GAMES

| DIRECTION OF RUN | GROUND COVERED | PASS | TRY LINE |
|---|---|---|---|

## IDEAL FOR IMPROVING PASSING AND HANDLING

### GAME NOTES

→ Set out a playing area with 2 teams of 4 players.

→ The aim is to make as many passes as possible without the 'Hungry Foxes' intercepting the ball.

→ If they intercept the ball they become the 'Hound'.

→ You cannot grab the ball from the 'Hound' just intercept it.

→ If you drop the ball or go outside the playing area, the other team gains possession.

### THE SET UP

→ 10m x 10m square.

→ 4 cones, a ball and four bibs.

→ 2 teams of 4.

### HOW TO SCORE?

→ 1 point for each completed pass.

### WHAT TO CALL OUT

→ "Keep the ball in two hands"

→ "Put your hands out as a target"

→ "Keep moving and look for space"

→ "Communicate and look for the pass"

### Coaching Notes

✔ Make sure that all players are moving into space to receive a pass.

✔ Get your players to communicate.

✔ Make it more difficult by reducing the number of 'Hounds' or 'Hungry Foxes'.

**1**

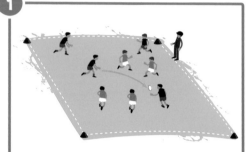

Set out a playing area with 2 teams of 4, to make as many passes as possible.

**2**

1 group of 'Hungry Foxes' must try to intercept the ball and become 'Hounds'.

**3**

You cannot grab the ball, you must intercept it and if you drop the ball you become a 'Fox'.

**4V4**  **12×12**

SMALL SIDED GAME
## TACKLE THE MONSTER

| DIRECTION OF RUN | GROUND COVERED | PASS | TRY LINE |
|---|---|---|---|

## IDEAL FOR IMPROVING TACKLING

## GAME NOTES

→ Select 2 teams of 4 players, each team with 1 tackler (the 'Monster') and 3 x 'Aliens'.

→ The 3 x 'Aliens' have to move and pass the ball amongst themselves.

→ While they are doing this the 'Monster' has to make as many tags or two-handed touch tackles as they can in 40 seconds.

→ As soon as an 'Alien' is tackled he must pass the ball to another 'Alien'.

## THE SET UP

→ 5m x 5m square.

→ 4 cones, a ball and one bib.

→ 2 teams of 4 with 1 defender and 3 attackers.

## HOW TO SCORE?

→ 1 point for each tackle made in 40 seconds.

## WHAT TO CALL OUT

→ "Keep the ball in two hands"

→ "Put your hands out as a target"

→ "Count the number of TACKLES out"

## Coaching Notes

✔ Make the playing area smaller if the tackler is not making enough tackles.

✔ Make sure every player gets to be a 'Monster'.

**1**

Create 2 teams of 4 - 1 tackler called a 'Monster' and 3 x 'Aliens' on each team.

**2**

Whilst the 'Aliens' are throwing the ball around, the 'Monster' must tag as many as possible.

**3**

If an 'Alien' is tagged, he must pass. The 'Monster' must tag as many 'Aliens'.

SMALL SIDED GAME
## Ghosts and Angels

4V3   10x10

| DIRECTION OF RUN | GROUND COVERED | PASS | TRY LINE |
|---|---|---|---|

## IDEAL FOR IMPROVING TACKLING

### GAME NOTES

➜ Create 2 in-goal areas at the end of the playing area.

➜ Divide the teams in fours with a 'Ghost' from each team standing in an in-goal area.

➜ Give the ball to one team (3 x 'Angels') and get them to pass it around.

➜ If an 'Angel' in possession is tackled, (tag or 2 handed touched) the ball is turned over.

➜ Players can knock down the ball or intercept it or if it is dropped they gain possession.

➜ Each player must touch the ball before giving it to the 'Ghost'.

### THE SET UP

➜ 10m x 10m square.

➜ 4 cones and a ball.

➜ 2 teams of 4 with 1 keeper and 3 attackers.

### HOW TO SCORE?

➜ 1 point for each pass made to the 'Angel'.

### WHAT TO CALL OUT

➜ "Pass to 'Angels' that are free"

➜ "Keep your hands out as a target"

➜ "Look at where the 'Angels' are going"

➜ Shout out number of TACKLES and TURNOVERS.

### Coaching Notes

✔ Get your players to anticipate what is likely to happen.

✔ Make sure plenty of communication is happening.

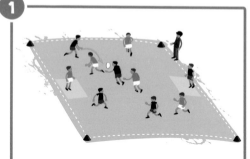

**1**

Divide the squad into teams of 4 with 1 player from each side remaining in an in-goal area.

**2**

If an 'Angel' is caught in possession, the ball is given to the 'Ghosts'.

**3**

If the ball is dropped, intercepted or knocked down, possession is given to the opposition.

**10x5**

| DIRECTION OF RUN | GROUND COVERED | PASS | TRY LINE |

## IDEAL FOR IMPROVING DECISION MAKING

## GAME NOTES

→ Get teams of 3 to line up at one end and a defender on the opposite end.

→ The attackers have 5 attempts to score a try by passing backwards only.

→ The attackers can dodge the defender, but must not be tackled or step out of bounds.

→ The attackers must decide to dodge, pass to score, while the defender must decide how to tackle.

→ Rotate the defender after 5 attempts.

## THE SET UP

→ 5m x 10m channel.

→ 4 cones and a ball.

→ The squad, divided in 3's verses a defender.

## HOW TO SCORE?

→ 1 point for each try.

→ 1 point for the best defender who stops a try.

## WHAT TO CALL OUT

→ "Play what is in front of you"

→ "Pass backwards either 'flat' or 'deep'"

→ "Anticipate what the ball-carrier will do"

→ "Communicate with your attackers"

## Coaching Notes

✔ Make sure they pass backwards.

✔ Make sure they decide and execute.

✔ Get them to move the ball to the middle so they have options both left and right.

✔ Narrow the channel if too easy to score.

**1**

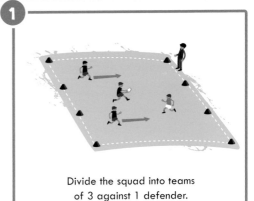

Divide the squad into teams of 3 against 1 defender.

**2**

The attackers must score a try by beating the defender and passing backwards only.

**3**

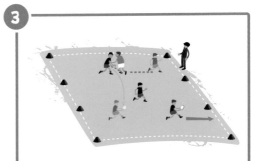

The defender must decide which attacker to tackle in order to prevent a try.

# RUGBY GAMES

16+    15x15

| DIRECTION OF RUN | GROUND COVERED | PASS | TRY LINE |
|---|---|---|---|

## IDEAL FOR IMPROVING DECISION MAKING

## GAME NOTES

➜ Divide the players into groups of 4.
➜ The groups jog around and they follow one another, while staying inside the playing area.
➜ Make sure they avoid crashing into each other.
➜ Each group has a ball and the lead player is closely followed by their team.
➜ The coach calls, "pop, pass, drop, place or roll" and the ball-carrier must carry out this instruction.
➜ Pop the ball to the right and the second player catches it, and so on to the last.
➜ Each time the player who plays the ball jogs to the back of the line.

## THE SET UP

➜ 15m x 15m.
➜ 4 cones and a ball.

## HOW TO SCORE?

➜ 1 point for each successful set of 4 drills.

## WHAT TO CALL OUT

➜ "POP" - the ball to the right.
➜ "PASS" - step right and pass the ball.
➜ "DROP" - to the ground and pick up the ball before all stepping over the fallen player.
➜ "PLACE" - the ball on the ground for picking up.
➜ "ROLL" - the ball on the ground for picking up.

## Coaching Notes

✔ Can be used as a warm-up.
✔ Pop the ball to the left, right or overhead.
✔ Eventually get the lead player to decide what to do with the ball.

**1**

Divide the squad into groups of 4 and get them to jog behind one another without crashing.

**2**

You instruct the lead player to 'pop', 'pass' 'drop', 'place' or 'roll' the ball.

**3**

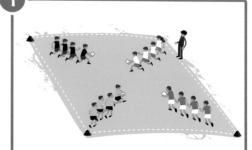

In tandem after each player carries out the instruction, they return to the back of the line.

## IDEAL FOR IMPROVING DECISION MAKING

### GAME NOTES

→ Assemble groups of 3 attackers against 3 defenders.

→ Space the defenders equally along the channel.

→ Defenders can only move sideways not forward.

→ Using skills they have acquired, the attackers must run or pass the 3 defenders without being tackled.

→ If the ball is dropped or a player steps outside the channel or is tackled, the mission as failed.

→ Change the tacklers after 9 or 10 defences.

### THE SET UP

→ 21m long x 7m wide.

→ 10 cones, a ball and tag belts if available.

### HOW TO SCORE?

→ 3 points for each successful try.

→ -1 point for each mission failure.

### WHAT TO CALL OUT

→ "Play what is in front of you"

→ "Pass backwards either 'flat' or 'deep'"

→ "Anticipate what the ball-carrier will do"

→ "Communicate with your fellow attackers"

→ "Run forward and commit the defender"

## Coaching Notes

✔ Encourage defenders to commit to the tackle.

✔ Ensure the ball-carrier makes his way to the middle, with options left and right.

✔ Encourage flair with dumpy passes.

✔ This can be increased to a 5v2's.

**1**

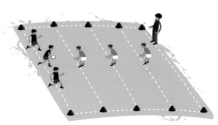

3 attackers play against 3 defenders in single file, thus creating a 3 v 1 situation.

**2**

Defenders can only move sideways while the attackers can only pass the ball backwards.

**3**

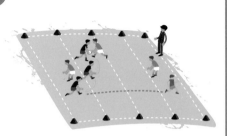

The mission fails if the player loses the ball in a tackle or the pass is forward or dropped.

# RUGBY GAMES

 4V4 | 10x12

| DIRECTION OF RUN | GROUND COVERED | PASS | TRY LINE |
| --- | --- | --- | --- |

## IDEAL FOR IMPROVING TEAM SKILLS

### GAME NOTES

→ Divide the players into teams of 4 or 5.
→ Teams start from the same base line and face in opposite direction.
→ Role the ball towards one end and shout "GO".
→ That team are now the attackers and they must run, pass, evade and use their skills to score a try.
→ If tackled, they have 3 seconds to pass the ball or the defenders win. They also win if the attackers step out of play, pass forward or drop the ball.
→ Give each team 2 or 3 attempts before mixing them up.

### THE SET UP

→ 12m long x 10m deep.
→ 4 cones and a ball.
→ 8 - 4 attackers and 4 defenders.

### HOW TO SCORE?

→ 2 points for each successful try.
→ 1 point for each successful defence.

### WHAT TO CALL OUT

→ "Play what is in front of you"
→ "Pass backwards and run forward"
→ "Support the ball-carrier"
→ "Communicate with your fellow attackers"

### Coaching Notes

✔ Make sure they number up against the attackers.
✔ Alter the playing area to suit your players' ability.
✔ Get the attackers to move into a backline formation quickly to receive a pass.

**1**

Line up your 4 attackers and 4 defenders along the same side line.

**2**

On your command the 2 groups run around a cone into the playing area.

**3**

You then throw the ball to an attacker and they must try score a try against the 4 defenders.

# RUGBY GAMES

## Games Suitable for Players Aged 10–13

## SMALL SIDED GAME
### Spot the Gap

6V4 | 75X24

DIRECTION OF RUN | GROUND COVERED | PASS | TRY LINE

## IDEAL FOR IMPROVING PASSING AND HANDLING

### GAME NOTES

→ Set out 3 Channels of equal width, but the middle channel has 2 defenders.

→ The game starts with 6 attackers players passing in an effort to beat the 4 defenders.

→ The attackers must stay in designated channels and draw the defenders to create a gap.

→ Passes must be backwards and dropped balls is penalised by deducting a try from the final count.

→ After a number of attempts change the players around.

### THE SET UP

→ 3 channels - 25m long x 8m deep.

→ 22 cones and a ball.

→ 10 - 6 attackers and 4 defenders.

### HOW TO SCORE?

→ Attackers are given 2 minutes to score as many tries as possible.

### WHAT TO CALL OUT

→ "Communicate your position to the ball-carrier"

→ "Move into space at speed"

→ "Hands out and ready to receive pass"

→ "Communicate with your fellow attackers where the space is likely to be"

### Coaching Notes

✔ Ensure the quality of the Pass opens up the Space.

✔ Progress by encouraging the use of the Skip Pass and Dummy Runner.

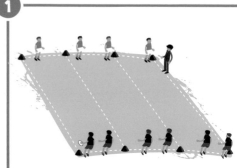

**1**

The game starts with 6 attackers trying to score a try against 4 defenders.

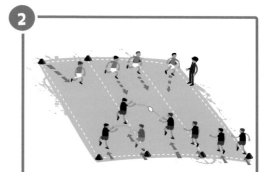

**2**

The defenders cannot cross a line of white cones in the middle of the playing area.

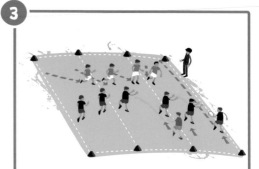

**3**

Attackers must stay in their designated channel and can only pass the ball backwards.

# RUGBY GAMES

**5V5** | **25X10**

SMALL SIDED GAME
## Machine Gun Passing

| DIRECTION OF RUN | GROUND COVERED | PASS | TRY LINE |
|---|---|---|---|

## IDEAL FOR IMPROVING PASSING AND HANDLING

### GAME NOTES

→ Set out a channel with 25 cones, 1 meter apart in a straight line.

→ The lead player races to the first cone and his partners go to the next 4 cones.

→ Each player passes backwards and then races to the next available cone up the line.

→ This is repeated until the team comes to the end of the line.

→ Play teams against each other to see who wins.

### THE SET UP

→ Set out a playing area 25m x 10m.

→ 25 cones and a ball.

→ 5 players passing left to right and 5 players passing right to left.

### HOW TO SCORE?

→ The team who reaches the opposite end and back again - wins.

### WHAT TO CALL OUT

→ Call out the time to put them under pressure.

→ "Ensure your hands are ready to accept the pass and in the correct position"

## Coaching Notes

✔ Communicate with one another.

✔ Make sure the passing is accurate.

✔ Increase the number of cones and number of players to suit your squad.

**1**

Place a row of cones 1m apart for approximately 25m.

**2**

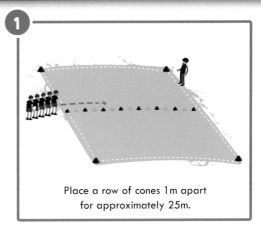

The lead player goes to the first cone and the other players go to the next 4 cones.

**3**

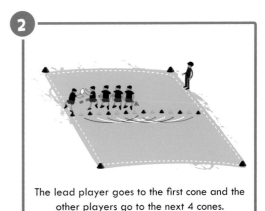

The ball is passed backward and the player who passing the ball joins the front of the line.

| DIRECTION OF RUN | GROUND COVERED | PASS | TRY LINE |
|---|---|---|---|

## IDEAL FOR IMPROVING PASSING AND HANDLING

### GAME NOTES

➔ Set out 4 cones 1 metre apart with a player standing on each cone.

➔ Moving out 12m set out 4 more cones and increase the space between the cones to 2m.

➔ Repeat this process and increase the distance between cones to 4m, 5.5m and 7m.

➔ Pass the ball across the line from cone to cone without the players moving.

### THE SET UP

➔ Set out a playing area 28m x 48m.

➔ 16 cones and a ball.

➔ Team of 4 race against one another.

### HOW TO SCORE?

➔ Against the clock get 4 players timed against each other.

### WHAT TO CALL OUT

➔ "Move the ball across the body"

➔ "Ensure the hands are ready to accept the pass and are in the correct position"

## Coaching Notes

✔ Adjust the distance to appropriate age and ability level.

✔ Progress to players passing while running.

✔ Progress further to skip passes.

✔ You can time the groups to see who is the fastest out and back.

**1**

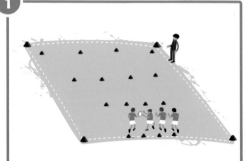

4 players start on 4 cones 1m apart and pass the ball back and forth along the line.

**2**

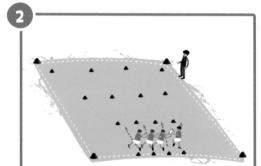

They move to the next set of cones which are now 4m apart and they pass to one another.

**3**

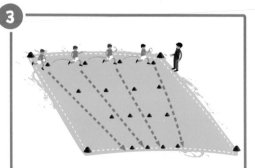

They continue to 5.5m and 7m, increasing the speed of the pass across the body.

SMALL SIDED GAME
## DANCING FEET

**IDEAL FOR IMPROVING AGILITY**

## GAME NOTES

→ Set out 4 ladders randomly around the square.
→ Start with 4 players running through a particular ladder at speed.
→ Whilst their partner jogs around the square, when they are finished they pass the ball and the roles reverse. Once completed they pass the ball to the next player and this is repeated for a specific time.

## THE SET UP

→ Set out a playing area 20m x 20m.
→ 4 cones, 4 ladders and a ball.
→ 4 players against 4 players.

## HOW TO SCORE?

→ Count the number of ladders a pair might complete over a set time period to determine the winners.

## WHAT TO CALL OUT

→ "Move on the balls of your feet"
→ "Keep your head up and keep both hands on the ball"
→ "No dropped passes and communicate"

## Coaching Notes

✔ Progress to each team having to move to a different or free ladder.
✔ Change the running style from stepping in every rung to feet in each rung or zigzag in and out of each rung.

**1**

Place 4 agility ladders randomly and get 4 players to pick up a ball to run through them.

**2**

The other players run outside the square and collect a pass when the other player is finished.

**3**

Continue this for 60 seconds and also vary the stepping style inside the ladder.

# RUGBY GAMES

6V6  30x25

DIRECTION OF RUN · GROUND COVERED · PASS · TRY LINE

## IDEAL FOR IMPROVING AGILITY

### GAME NOTES

→ Set out 5 tackle bags or 5 tubes at one end of the playing area.

→ Set out 5 defenders opposite 5 attackers and on your whistle they race towards the gates.

→ The attacker has a split-second to decide on which side to run and evade being tackled.

→ A tackle is made with a two-handed touch.

→ Change defenders to attackers and vice versa.

### THE SET UP

→ Set out a playing area 30m x 25m.

→ 4 cones, 5 tackle bags and a ball.

→ 5 players against 5 players.

### HOW TO SCORE?

Count the number of tries scored by one team against the other.

### WHAT TO CALL OUT

→ "Move on the balls of your feet"

→ "Keep an eye on the defender to gain an advantage"

→ "Make your decision quickly"

## Coaching Notes

✔ Give a shorter distance to attackers if scoring tries is proving difficult.

✔ This will also get them to the ball earlier.

**1**

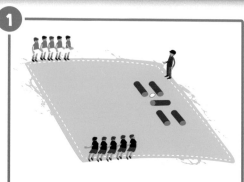

Set up 2 tackle gates with an exit either right or left, and 2 teams of 5 on either side.

**2**

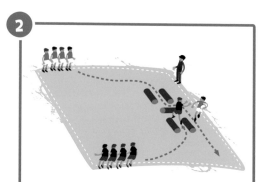

On your whistle, the first defender and attacker race to the tubes to defend or score a try.

**3**

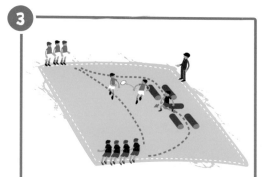

After a couple of attempts swap the roles and/or send in a second attacker to create a 2v1.

**5v5**  **20x20**

| DIRECTION OF RUN | GROUND COVERED | PASS | TRY LINE |
|---|---|---|---|

## IDEAL FOR IMPROVING TACKLING

### GAME NOTES

➜ Line up 5 players facing 5 players.

➜ Place a matching coloured cone equidistant to the left and right of the centre line of players.

➜ Call a particular colour and the ball-carrier must run outside that cone without his opposite player tackling them.

➜ The ball-carrier decides if they run to the left or right cone.

➜ Don't allow the attacker to run outside the next coloured cone to avoid being tackled.

### THE SET UP

➜ Set out a playing area 20m x 20m.

➜ 2 x 4 different coloured cones (red, yellow, white and green) and 5 balls.

➜ 5 players against 5 players.

### HOW TO SCORE?

Count the number of tries scored by one team against the other.

### WHAT TO CALL OUT

➜ "Watch the first movement of the ball-carrier"

➜ "Get your feet close to your opponent to make a good tackle"

➜ "Make your decision quickly to gain an advantage"

### Coaching Notes

✔ Progress to the tackler getting up to his feet quickly to contest the ball.

**1**

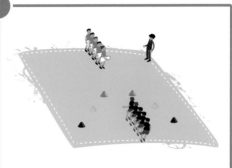

A 5-a-side game with equal attackers and defenders with each attacker having a ball.

**2**

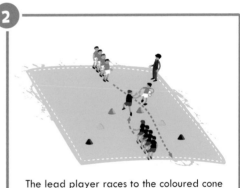

The lead player races to the coloured cone you call out, and they must score a try.

**3**

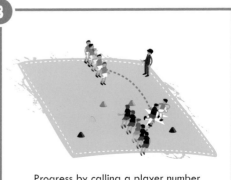

Progress by calling a player number and a coloured cone to begin the attack.

# RUGBY GAMES

1v1    8x8

| DIRECTION OF RUN | GROUND COVERED | PASS | TRY LINE |

## IDEAL FOR IMPROVING TACKLING

### GAME NOTES

→ Get 2 players to stand back-to-back to one another.

→ Place a ball 5m to their right, on your command, they must compete for the ball and then race around the cone and enter the square at one end while the other player enters the square at the opposite end.

→ The ball-carrier must try to score a try while the opposite player must try to stop them.

→ You can make it touch tackle, two-handed or full contact, depending on ability.

→ Don't allow the attacker to run outside the next coloured cone to avoid being tackled.

### THE SET UP

→ Set out a playing area 8m x 8m.

→ 2 cones and a ball.

→ 1 v 1.

### HOW TO SCORE?

→ Count the number of tries scored and the number of tackles made.

### WHAT TO CALL OUT

→ "Get your feet close to your opponent to make a good tackle"

→ "Use quick feet to avoid being tackled"

### Coaching Notes

✔ Progress to introduce additional defenders and attackers. This will result in a 2 v 1 or 3 v 2 etc.

**1**

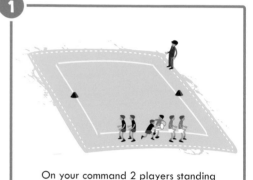

On your command 2 players standing back-to-back race around a cone to compete.

**2**

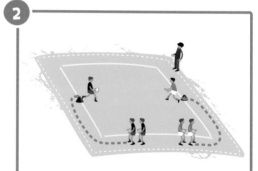

The attacker must try to evade the tackle and the defender must avoid a try being scored.

**3**

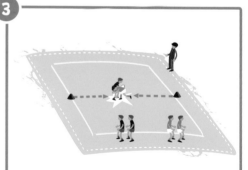

Start this game by getting the players to grapple for the ball to determine the attacker.

4V2 | 25X12

**SMALL SIDED GAME**
## Hands Free

DIRECTION OF RUN | GROUND COVERED | PASS | TRY LINE

## IDEAL FOR IMPROVING TACKLING

## GAME NOTES

→ Get 2 defenders to hold tackle bags and 5 attackers to control the ball.

→ The attackers pass the ball around the small area and avoid being hit with a tackle bag, whilst in possession.

→ On your command, the tackle bags are dropped and the 2 defenders race to defend the try line of the larger playing area.

→ The 5 attackers race to the other line to begin a 5 v 2.

## THE SET UP

→ Set out two playing areas, one 10m x 5m and a larger area measuring 15m x 12m.

→ 7 cones, 2 tackle bags and a ball.

→ 5 v 2.

## HOW TO SCORE?

→ 2 Points for a try.

→ 1 point for a successful pass out of a tackle.

→ -1 for a tackle without off-loading.

## WHAT TO CALL OUT

→ "Keep your hands high to get a pass away"

→ "Get your feet close to your opponent to make a good tackle"

→ "Communicate with one another"

### coaching Notes

✔ Decrease it to 3 v 2 to improve decision making and promote tackling.

✔ Make sure the ball is carried in both hands.

**1**

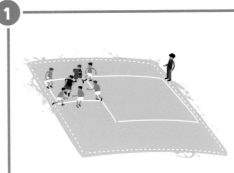

5 attackers pass the ball around whilst 2 defenders tackle them with tackle pads.

**2**

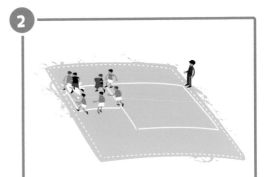

On the whistle the defenders drop the tackle pads and race to defend the try line.

**3**

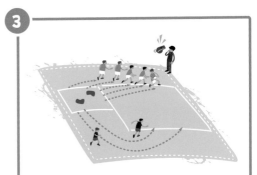

The 5 attackers must run to the opposite end and begin a 5 v 2 and score a try.

# RUGBY GAMES

4V4　12x30

| DIRECTION OF RUN | GROUND COVERED | PASS | TRY LINE |
|---|---|---|---|

## IDEAL FOR IMPROVING TEAM SKILLS

### GAME NOTES

➜ Set out the playing area with 4 players in each channel.

➜ The first 2 players sprint down the channel, weaving through the slalom poles and passing to each other, as illustrated.

➜ When they reach the opposite end they sprint to the start position and pass the ball to their team.

➜ The next two mirror the drill and the game ends when the last pair complete the game.

### THE SET UP

➜ Set out 2 playing channels 12m x 30m.

➜ 4 x cones, 2 x tackle pads, 19 x slalom poles and a ball.

➜ 4 v 4.

### HOW TO SCORE?

➜ The first team back to the start wins.

➜ Add 5 seconds for dropped balls or forward passes.

### WHAT TO CALL OUT

➜ "Keep both hands on the ball at all times"

➜ "Hands out and ready to receive pass"

➜ "No dropped balls and communicate"

## Coaching Notes

✔ This can be changed to 6 v 6 or increased to 8 v 8.

✔ This game can also help with your team's fitness, whilst enjoying the game.

**1**

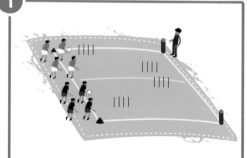

2 teams line up to run through a channel whilst passing and weaving through slalom poles.

**2**

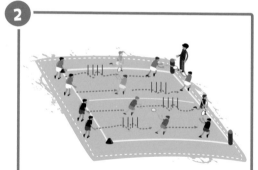

When they reach the opposite end they sprint around a tackle tube and return the ball.

**3**

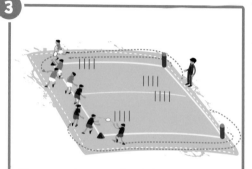

The next pair repeat the drill to determine the winning team after both teams are finished.

Games Suitable

for Players

Aged 14–16

**SMALL SIDED GAME**
## Sit it Out

8V4    35x20

DIRECTION OF RUN | GROUND COVERED | PASS | TRY LINE

## IDEAL FOR IMPROVING PASSING AND HANDLING

### GAME NOTES

➜ Set out the playing area with 4 tackle tubes at each corner, numbered 1 to 4.

➜ Start your players jogging around it, whilst they have one hand touching the tube at all times.

➜ On your command the team number called out sits down and the odd or even numbered team become defenders and the others attackers.

➜ Give a set time to score a try.

### THE SET UP

➜ Set out a playing area 35m x 20m.

➜ 4 x cones, 4 x tackle tubes and two balls.

➜ 8 v 4.

### HOW TO SCORE?

➜ Count the number of tries by each team.

➜ You can also award points for tries stopped.

### WHAT TO CALL OUT

➜ "Communicate with each other"

➜ "Get the ball into the centre to give options left and right"

➜ "No dropped balls and Listen to your team-mates"

### Coaching Notes

✔ Vary the numbers to suit your team ability.

✔ Game gives players the chance to move from attacking to defending quickly.

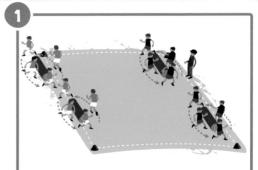

**1**

Players start by jogging around a tackle tube located and numbered at each corner.

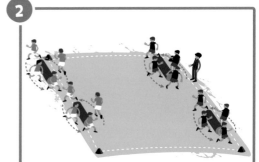

**2**

Whilst keeping a hand on it at all times, a number is called out and that team sits down.

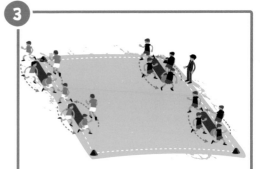

**3**

The team opposite those sitting become 4 defenders and the other 8 become attackers.

SMALL SIDED GAME
## circle of friends

| DIRECTION OF RUN | GROUND COVERED | PASS | TRY LINE |

## IDEAL FOR IMPROVING AGILITY

## GAME NOTES

→ Set out the playing area with a player trying to get the ball from his opponent whilst they run around a tackle tube.

→ On your call the ball-carrier throws the ball to the team they are facing, who are now 4 attackers.

→ Both players running around the tube now become 'friends' and defend the opposite end.

→ This now creates a 4 v 2.

## THE SET UP

→ Set out a playing square area 20m x 20m.

→ 4 x cones, 1 x tackle tube and a ball.

→ 4 v 2.

## HOW TO SCORE?

→ Count the number of tries by each team.

→ You can also award points for tries stopped.

## WHAT TO CALL OUT

→ "Communicate and listen to your team-mates instruction"

→ "Hands out and ready to receive pass"

→ "No dropped balls"

→ "Get in tight and make the tackle"

## Coaching Notes

✔ Get the player in the middle to pass it to the attacker placed out wide to encourage them to get the ball to the attackers in the middle.

✔ Increase or decrease the number of attackers and add an additional defender from the opposite try line.

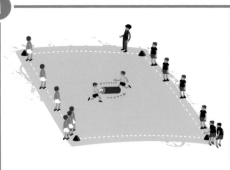

In teams of 4, a member of each team jogs around a tackle tube in the middle.

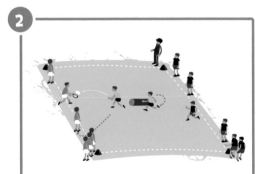

On your call, the attacker, who has a ball, throws it to the team he is facing to attack.

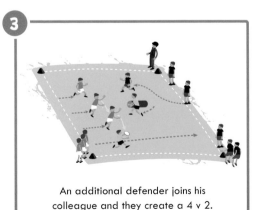

An additional defender joins his colleague and they create a 4 v 2.

# RUGBY GAMES

## SMALL SIDED GAME
## Down the Drainpipe

6V6 | 30x30

| DIRECTION OF RUN | GROUND COVERED | PASS | TRY LINE |

**IDEAL FOR IMPROVING TACKLING**

## GAME NOTES
→ Set up 2 teams of 5 attackers and 5 defenders.
→ Call the channels A, B and C.
→ And, call out a number of attackers to attack and the defenders must defend with one less in order to prevent a try.
→ Without being touch tackled the attackers must score a try.

## THE SET UP
→ Set out a playing area of 30m x 30m with 3 channels of 10m wide.
→ 12 x cones and a ball.
→ Up to 6 v 6.

## HOW TO SCORE?
→ Each team must try to score a try.
→ The points awarded for a try is the number of attackers left on the try line.
→ Defenders get 2 points for preventing a try.

## WHAT TO CALL OUT
→ "Decide on the number of defenders you need"
→ "No dropped balls"
→ "Get in tight and make the tackle"
→ "Communicate with one another"

### Coaching Notes
✔ Move to full contact, if necessary.
✔ Make sure that good decisions are being made by both defenders and attackers.

**1**

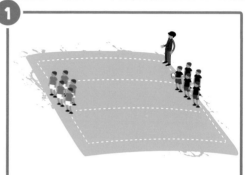

2 teams of 5 face each other in front of 3 clearly marked numbered channels.

**2**

You shout 'B3' - indicating the channel and the number of attackers to attack.

**3**

Following the number of attackers called '3', now 2 defenders must prevent a try.

130

**3V2**  **40x12**

| DIRECTION OF RUN | GROUND COVERED | PASS | TRY LINE |
|---|---|---|---|

## IDEAL FOR IMPROVING TACKLING

### GAME NOTES

➜ Set out a channel and divide it into 4 coloured segments with cones.

➜ With 2 defenders and 3 attackers, an attacker kicks the ball into a dominated coloured zone and the 3 attackers collect the ball and score a try between the coloured cones you referenced.

➜ Once they score the try the defenders enter the channel to defend the base line to stop a try being scored.

### THE SET UP

➜ Set out a 10m x 40m channel.

➜ 8 (2 x 4) coloured cones and a ball.

➜ 3 v 2.

### HOW TO SCORE?

➜ Three points for every try scored.

➜ One point for every try stopped.

➜ Each individual keeps his score.

### WHAT TO CALL OUT

➜ "Hold the ball in both hands"

➜ "No dropped balls and tackle in tight"

➜ "Communicate with those around you"

### coaching Notes

✔ Vary the tackle from tip, to both hands touching to full contact.

✔ Increase the width to accommodate a 4 v 3 or a 5 v 4.

**1**

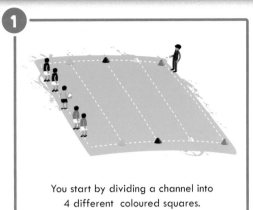

You start by dividing a channel into 4 different coloured squares.

**2**

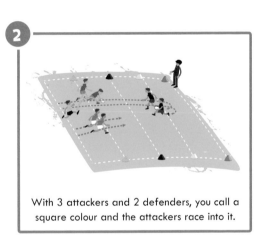

With 3 attackers and 2 defenders, you call a square colour and the attackers race into it.

**3**

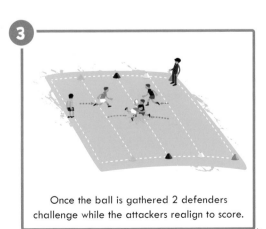

Once the ball is gathered 2 defenders challenge while the attackers realign to score.

**131**

SMALL SIDED GAME
## Strike the Posts

1v1  22x15

| DIRECTION OF RUN | GROUND COVERED | PASS | TRY LINE |
|---|---|---|---|

## IDEAL FOR IMPROVING KICKING SKILLS

### GAME NOTES

➜ Lay down 2 lines of cones and balls at 5, 10, 15, 22 and 25m from the try line, in line with the goal posts.

➜ Get 2 players to pass to a kicker, who will try and grubber kick the ball and hit his goal post.

➜ Starting from the 5m cone, it becomes more difficult as they move farther away.

### THE SET UP

➜ Set out 2 playing channels 12m x 30m.

➜ 10 x cones and 10 balls.

➜ 1 v 1.

### HOW TO SCORE?

➜ 5 points for hitting the post.

➜ Add 1 point from each cone position the farther they go out.

### WHAT TO CALL OUT

➜ "Make sure the pass is accurate"

➜ "Hands out and fingers spread to receive pass"

➜ "Quick look at the target before kicking"

➜ "Drop the ball on to your boot laces to kick"

## Coaching Notes

✔ Ideal for improving the skills of a scrumhalf and outhalf.

✔ Make it harder by increasing distance from passer to kicker.

✔ Increase the pressure on the kicker by timing him to finish the game.

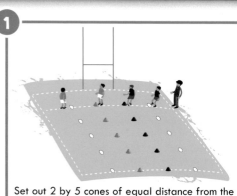

**1**

Set out 2 by 5 cones of equal distance from the goal posts, with a kicker on the first cone.

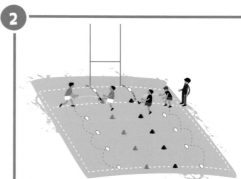

**2**

A player stands at a cone 5m away, to pass a ball to the kicker who attempts to hit the post.

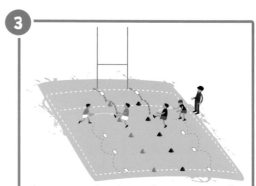

**3**

In a race against time and to score points for accuracy the pass and kicks must be good.

SMALL SIDED GAME
## Out the Gap

| DIRECTION OF RUN | GROUND COVERED | PASS | TRY LINE |
|---|---|---|---|

## IDEAL FOR IMPROVING KICKING SKILLS

### GAME NOTES

➜ From the try line, get a team of 4 players to relay to each position and kick the ball through the cones.

➜ Only after the ball has travelled past the cones can the next player race to his ball and kick.

➜ Each team has 3 attempts to score as many points as possible.

### THE SET UP

➜ Place 2 cones 25m apart at 4 different points (10m, 20m, 30m and 40m).

➜ 6 x cones and 9 balls.

➜ 4 v 4.

### HOW TO SCORE?

➜ 2, 3 and 4 points are awarded for each gap based on increased difficulty.

➜ Add 3 points to the fastest team.

### WHAT TO CALL OUT

➜ "Quick look at the target before kicking"

➜ "Drop the ball on to your boot laces to kick"

## Coaching Notes

✔ Vary the distance kicked depending on ability.

✔ Decrease the size of the gap to challenge the players.

✔ Vary the kick from 'Grubber' to 'Chip' to 'Up and Unders'.

✔ You can also have 4 balls at each station and get all players to try to tread the ball through the different cones.

**1**

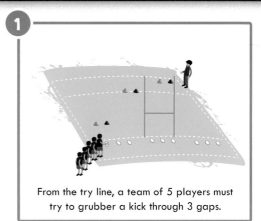

From the try line, a team of 5 players must try to grubber a kick through 3 gaps.

**2**

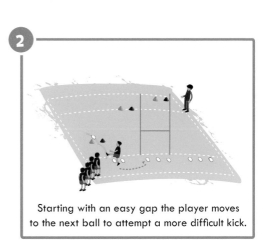

Starting with an easy gap the player moves to the next ball to attempt a more difficult kick.

**3**

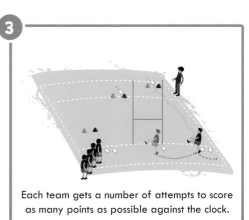

Each team gets a number of attempts to score as many points as possible against the clock.

# NOTES